W

WIZDOMTALK
THE DREAMMAKER

UNLEASH YOUR VISION!

By PRINCE CHAZAQ

The DreamMaker Club Publishers

www.DreamMakerClub.org

Copyright © 2020 by Prince Chazaq

Cover illustration and design by Julio Sarita

ISBN: 978-0-578-24171-5

All rights reserved. No part of this book may be used or reproduced in any manner whatsoever without written permission, except for brief quotations embodied in critical articles and reviews. For more information, please address The DreamMaker Club Publishers.

The DreamMaker Club Publishers paperback printing: December 2020. WizdomTalk, The DREAMMAKER, Unleash Your Vision™ are trademarks of Prince Chazaq.

Printed in the United States of America

If you purchase this book without a cover, you should be aware that this book is stolen property. Neither the author nor the publisher has received any payment for this stripped book. "Books" published by The DreamMaker Club Publishers are available at the quantity discounts on bulk purchases for premium, educational, fund-raising, and special sales use. For details, please contact www.DreamMakerclub.org.

ACKNOWLEDGEMENTS

Tina Rasheed MS, Cynthia Snipes MSA, Chaplin Dale Felix BA, Clea de Moraes PhD, Cheryl Rush Dix MS, Verna Dwyer CEMPA, Dr. Peter Eche, Vanessa Beltran MA, and life coach Linda Gomes are among the academics I would like to thank for their help. I would also like to thank the communities of the Northern Mariana Islands, Guam, Federated States of Micronesia Islands, Palau, the United Arab Emirates, Nigeria, Egypt, Iraq, India, France, Germany, Rwanda, United Kingdom, Qatar, Singapore, Brazil, Japan, and the Dominican Republic for inspiring this book and serving as a source of learning.

FOREWORD

An evil Babylonian Cartel led by Dark Shadows is plotting to release a pandemic using unsuspecting global youth. The Cartel wants to control the people of the world and sabotage their dreams and ambitions. However, in the first Gulf War's backdrop and despair, a mysterious chest will appear in modern Sumer's desert. The soldiers, scholars, and villagers who stumble upon this chest will encounter a mystic Master Sage called WizdomTalk. He teaches wisdom, virtues, values, and character through fables. He will confront the evil Cartel in a dramatic showdown and prove that ALL LIVES MATTER!

BLESSING,
PRINCE CHAZAQ

DEDICATION

This book is dedicated to the Most High, their creation, and my legacy Lisa Marie, Precious Princess, and Dr. Hezekiah II.

BLESSINGS!
PRINCE CHAZAQ

PART 1:
TABLE OF CONTENTS

PART I 11
Samaná Peninsula..12
The Babylonian Cartel 16
Port of Hamad - Qatar 26
Sumer, The Beginning....................................31
The Antiquities Mission 33
Underachievers...36
The Bedouins..38
Peppermint Chest...40
The Dark Shadows 46
Arrested Development 49
Wisdom 53
You Were Born a Winner 57
You Have a Purpose......................................60
You are a Work of Art...................................63
You Have Power!...65

The Power of Your Words..67
You Define Your Image 70
You are Extraordinarily Gifted.....................................73
Society's Leadership Roles 76
Micronesia 79
Major General Bain...83
Unleash Your Vision 85
Be a DREAMMAKER...90
Imaginative Creativity 92
What is your Dream? 96
Millennium Park...98

PART 2:
TABLE OF CONTENTS

PART II 101
Valley of the Kings 102
Controlled Opposition 104
Ingrid and El Marco 109
Year – 2035 112
Saipan 118
You are Beautiful Islands 126
Banzai Cliff: A Choice 128
Tools for Goal Setting 133
Planning 137
Time Management 140
A Balanced Sumo Wins! 142
Success is a Personal 145
The Drumbeats 148
The Palauan's Courage 151
The Refaluwasch – Education 155

It is All About Respect	159
A Bolt of Excellence	168
Our Compassion	171
Practice Stewardship	175
Something Greater Than You?	178
You are a Brand	183
The Debt Chains	186
Recognize Wealth around You	190
Life's ABCDs!	194
How Do I Have Prosperity?	199
Life's "L" Factors	208
About the Author	215

W

WIZDOMTALK
THE DREAMMAKER

UNLEASH YOUR VISION!

By PRINCE CHAZAQ

PART I

SAMANÁ PENINSULA

The Samaná Peninsula is located northeast of the lively, historic cities of Santo Domingo and Santiago. Huge, majestic waves pound the pristine, golden-sand beaches of the Dominican Republic in this sparkling paradise. Christopher Columbus, the explorer, gave the island the name 'Insula Hispaniola' which in Latin means the Spanish Island. Near the Caribbean Sea's deep blue ocean, the Peninsula hides its exotic lush, palm-filled jungles, humpback whales, and caverns. For the wealthy and powerful, this protected harbor of coconut plantations and secluded rain forests is a well-kept secret.

The Samaná-Americans live in the Samaná Peninsula. These people are descended from freed African American slaves who arrived in the Dominican Republic in 1824.

The Samaná-Americans preserve 19th-century African American culture's English language, names, traditions, food, and music. Their culture evolved because of their isolation from the rest of the Spanish-speaking Dominicans and French Creole-speaking Haitians on the island.

Boris Kligoff, a retired Russian colonel, relaxes on his white velvet lounge chair at the western extremity of the Samaná Peninsula. He surrounds himself with amusing and inquisitive visitors. He is wearing checkered shorts and is getting a warm cinnamon oil foot massage. Colonel Kligoff has reached the age of seventy and is balding. Despite this, the former career soldier maintains a powerful physique. He is fortunate to live on the Samaná Peninsula and possesses a gorgeous luxury villa. Ravi, the Raven, his assistant, is resting near him under a tall green mango tree.

The temperature in the Caribbean is unquestionably more pleasant than Russia's bitterly cold winters. The colonel's Caribbean paradise is the Royal Palace Estates. It is an upscale neighborhood with ultra-luxurious homes. Olympic-sized pools, beautiful green landscape, personal cooks, and massage therapists are among the attractions. There was also a private airstrip and a large staff to cater to every owner's desire.

The super-rich and mega-celebrities own these magnificent homes. El Marco, an eccentric global pop music sensation and movie star is one of the colonel's neighbors. A former Norwegian head of state is also a resident.

The phone suddenly rings, and the colonel answers. Lizette, a powerful member of a secret cartel, is on the other end of the line. She needed to confirm the colonel's plan to meet with the Cartel about the World Youth Summit 20/25 in Abuja, Nigeria.

His mind wandered as he listened on the phone while Maria and his house servants handed pineapple, strawberry, and mango beverages to his visitors. The colonel gives them a kind smile. Colonel Kligoff treats his servants as if they were family and pays them well. He holds the Dominican people in high regard and enjoys their cuisine, culture, and Latin music. He loves dancing the Merengue with the island's beautiful and voluptuous women. These women have a Spanish, African, and Taino Native American ancestry, as well as exotic skin tones.

The Samaná Peninsula is a tranquil and lonely location, yet the colonel still enjoys the excitement and intrigue of espionage as a former decorated military intelligence officer. Whale watching, forest excursions, and jaw-dropping dives at the El Limón waterfall are among the colonel's favorite activities. He enjoys riding his horse along the beach and he often zip lines through the jungle. Los Haitises National Park is one of his favorite places to visit because it protects one of the island's few remaining rainforests.

Colonel Kligoff, on the other hand, is preoccupied with something else today. The colonel is dreading his next meeting with the Cartel, which he had hoped to avoid. He is their chief spymaster. The colonel's monetary rewards and special privileges were insufficient to compensate for his total contempt for the Cartel and its methods.

The colonel looks up to the sky and notices that it is darkening. He changes the dial on his television to a weather channel, where he learns that a super cyclone is rapidly shifting paths. The hurricane was now around the countries of Haiti and the Dominican Republic.

Ravi is startled awake by the colonel's loud whistle. He tells Ravi to go to Abuja to deliver essential information to Lizette concerning the World Youth Summit 20/25 and the near fatal Meta-Mutate Virus (MetaMutate-25). Ravi bows to his boss and gets ready for the long voyage ahead of him. High winds begin to blow swiftly later in the evening, and thunder and lightning bolts begin to fracture the sky. Every communication to and from the outside world is off within hours.

The colonel is overjoyed that he would not be able to attend the meeting in West Africa. Colonel Kligoff considers the forty-nine cartel members who will gather in Africa, as well as his vacant chair. The colonel enjoys a Cuban cigar while sipping Russian vodka and smiling mischievously like a child. He started to laugh as he remembered the mysterious persona WizdomTalk, whom he had met years ago in a place once known as *Sumer*.

THE BABYLONIAN CARTEL

On a quiet night in Abuja, Nigeria, black crows squawk while the streets stay deserted. Around midnight, sleek, self-driving Rolls Royce limousines arrive at the Five-Star Transcorp Hilton Hotel, directed by global positioning system (GPS) navigation satellites. The premium hotel has a view of an eight-million-person metropolis. At least for some people, this modern Mecca is a symbol of Africa's might and riches.

The origins of the cartel can be traced back to ancient Babylon or Sumer in the Middle Eastern region. "Order out of Chaos" was their motto.

Other cartel members will attend the meeting virtually, as holograms in a variety of hues, via cyberspace. Each person took a seat. A few of the world's wealthiest and most powerful people are members of this group. These cartel members were present at the World Summit 20/25 for world leaders on economics, education, innovation, health, and peace. The Babylonian Cartel, on the other hand, was more preoccupied with the World Youth Summit 20/25. The summit will take place in Egypt's Valley of the Kings in a few weeks.

The purpose of the big event is to inspire and empower the youth of the world. Why are these powerful people concerned about the future of the world's youth? They agree that youth are the future, and they want to rule them. At this Summit, all the world's nations would send their best and brightest young people. With the Cartel's goal disguised in the facts and lessons gathered at this outstanding event, the Babylonian Cartel hopes to influence them.

The Summit will be broadcasted to billions of young people around the world via television and the internet. Youth leaders aged 17 to 25 will unwittingly return to their home countries and implement the Babylonian Cartel's beliefs and plans.

The main issue of the Cartel's special meeting was WizdomTalk, the keynote speaker at the World Youth Summit 20/25. He is a powerful, wise, and ageless Sage. The nasty cartel referred to him as a bumbling rogue and despised him vehemently. The cartel is aware that WizdomTalk has the power to smash the cartel's terrible plan for the youth.

They saw that WizdomTalk had the potential to affect young people. Not only because of his wonderful WIZDOMPOWER ideology, but also because of the considerable media attention he will receive. Members of the cartel did not want this to happen.

"Where is WizdomTalk now?" asked Constantine, a cunning cartel member. The Raven, Ravi, was the first to respond to the question.

"Colonel Boris Kligoff has requested that I report to all of you. WizdomTalk will travel to Qatar's port of Hamad next week, according to our intelligence gathering contacts on the ground. He then intends to travel to the Mariana Islands by ship to see his former protégé, Major General Bain. He will talk to the Islanders and their visitors at a festival once he arrives. WizdomTalk, also, intends to speak at the World Youth Summit 20/25 by satellite from Saipan, rather than in person."

Lizzette, a member of the Cartel, stated, "Oh my goodness! So, this jerk is not going to show up in person? We will have plenty of time to plan for this character's end now. We will turn off all communications from the islands before WizdomTalk speaks. Because we dominate the worldwide media, this will be a simple task for us. Ravi has done an outstanding job. Thank you very much."

Lizette slammed her hands against the conference table so hard that her artificial fingernails cracked, and her dirty dentures slipped out of her mouth. She screams passionately, toothless, "WIZDOMTALK, THIS

IMBECILE, MUST NEVER BE ALLOWED TO TELL THE WORLD'S YOUTH WHO THEY ARE. HE MUST BE UNABLE TO REVEAL THEIR POWER AND VISION! HE MUST NEVER BE ABLE TO TEACH ANYONE HOW TO USE THIS KNOWLEDGE, BECAUSE IF HE DOES, OUR WEALTH, POWER, AND PLANS WILL BE DESTRUCTED!"

Lizette is self-conscious about her fake nails and false teeth, so she recovers them apologetically. "What is next on the agenda?" she inquired, still seething over WizdomTalk. The Cartel's other plan is to have its agents inject MetaMutate-25, a lethal, time-released virus, into the gift bags of all World Youth Summit 20/25 attendees. This virus is as deadly as the 1918 Spanish flu epidemic, which killed fifty-four million people worldwide. MetaMutate-25 affected people can have the virus for up to 14 days before showing symptoms. Fever, fatigue, a dry cough, and shortness of breath are the most prevalent MetaMutate-25 symptoms.

Most patients can recover from their sickness without requiring any specific therapy. On the other hand, the illness could be catastrophic, even fatal. People who are older or have medical conditions such as asthma, diabetes, or heart disease are more likely to fall ill. The Cartel's purpose is to spread the virus over the world when the youth return home with contaminated gift bags. The vaccination that will cure the infection is patented by the Cartel.

The MetaMutate-25 disaster would wreak devastation on the world's economies, social institutions, and freedom of travel in general.

The Cartel would appear as a rescuer, claiming to have discovered a treatment for the deadly sickness. The vaccination will be sold to governments at a huge profit, according to the Cartel's strategy. This would significantly increase their ill-gotten gains in cash. The Babylonian Cartel was overjoyed with their strategy, agreed completely with it, and began to rejoice.

They partied wildly, abusing narcotics, consuming enormous amounts of alcohol, and engaging in dangerous behaviors without restraint.

The stench of sulfur became unbearable suddenly. This was a forewarning that the Cartel's boss was on his way. They expected him to be filthy and stinky as usual. The Cartel members laugh and hold their noses as they wait for their leader to reveal their strategy.

Unleash Your Vision

The five-star Transcorp Hilton Hotel in Abuja, which is where the Babylonian Cartel meetings are held, is opulent. Expensive furniture, as well as artwork and exotic plants, adorned the conference area. There were fifty handcrafted mahogany chairs in the room. There were only two empty seats in the whole place.

Minutes later, there is a loud tap on the door, and the incredibly offensive odor grows stronger. A cartel member opens the door. The dirty odor was so strong that they all collapsed, and the plants died instantly. After recovering, members of the Babylonian Cartel cover their noses and laugh hysterically as they warmly welcome Dark Shadows.

With his crafty techniques, Dark Shadows serves them well, and they became very wealthy and successful. The deranged and wicked apparition sits down in his chair once all the hugs and greetings are gone, but one chair remains empty.

Dark Shadows' mouth opens. His breath has a sewer-like odor to it. Members of the cartel begin to vomit due to his green-yellow discolored teeth. Dark Shadows was unconcerned about this because he enjoys being nasty. "First and foremost, where is Colonel Boris Kligoff?" he inquires.

Lizette responds quickly "I spoke with him a few days ago, and he confirmed that he would be attending our meeting. However, we currently believe he will be unable to attend due to the Super Hurricane disrupting transit on the island."

Dark Shadows says, "Let us go ahead and proceed. We have a problem, people. As you may be aware, WizdomTalk, our archenemy, has been invited to appear at the World Youth Summit 20/25 as the keynote speaker for the youth. At all costs, we must not allow this man to speak."

Dark Shadows is interrupted by Tosaka, which is not a good thing to do. He is a newcomer to this nefarious organization. He slams his fist on the table and yells, "We are all multi-billionaires and powerful people seated here. Governments and international banks are under our power. We have a monopoly on big industries. We use troops against those who oppose our global goal, such as our opponents. I am new to this group and do not know everything there is to know about our past. What unique abilities does this WizdomTalk have in comparison to the powerful Babylonian Cartel? Let us now inflict physical injury on him."

Unleash Your Vision

Tosaka is anticipating a standing ovation for his inspiring remarks. However, the other cartel members, simply stared at Tosaka, perplexed. They asserted, "We attempted to harm WizdomTalk multiple times but were unsuccessful. Colonel Boris Kligoff, our greatest and deadliest operative, who would be sitting in this vacant chair today, has attempted to harm WizdomTalk more than twenty times over the years."

Then Lizette spoke up and reported for the cartel members to Dark Shadows. "Sir, our monitoring team has determined that WizdomTalk will not be present at the event. He will deliver his remarks to the Summit via satellite from the Saipan in the Mariana Islands. So, right before they unveil him as the Summit's keynote speaker, we propose that we disrupt all communications from the islands."

"Tosaka, I appreciate your excitement," Dark Shadows replied with a smile. He slaps the new cartel member for interrupting him and being so naive.

The deranged personality then raises his hand to the heavens and exclaims, "WizdomTalk is a Master Sage, so remember that. He is a mystic and an expert teacher. He possesses remarkable abilities bestowed by The Most High. WizdomTalk's actions are driven by noble intentions. Truth, faith, creativity, freedom of thought, compassion, and constructive behaviors are the weapons he wields."

Dark Shadows then points below and talks once more, "We are given power by the Most Below, and our intentions are terrible. Deception, fear, manipulation, greed, wealth, and power are the weapons we use.

Thank you, Lizette; but your concept is far too simple for WizdomTalk; however, we will consider incorporating it into a more inventive plan. The plan to employ MetaMutate-25 is, however, fantastic!"

Andy, a shrewd member of the cartel who spoke up, "Hey, I have got an idea. Let us include one of our friends, El Marco, a legendary celebrity musician and movie star, in the speaker roster. He is quite attractive, has a large international youth following, is well-dressed, and has a clean image and decent manners."

Another member of the Babylonian Cartel speaks up, "El Marco is weird, uneducated, and not particularly talkative. Do you think he will be able to stick to our agenda's objectives?"

After discussing El Marco with Dark Shadows and the other members, they agree to reconsider the proposal. They called the conference to a close and agreed to reconvene in the coming weeks to accomplish their destructive agenda. They decided to meet again in Abuja, this time at Millennium Park, which is a cool, open-air environment.

Basa, the hotel's housekeeper, comes over to clean the room after the cartel members have left in the afternoon.

Unleash Your Vision

She discovers a sizable payment for her services, and the room is peppermint scented. She also notices a dashing, ill-dressed man snoring as he slept. He has a wide smile on his face, his nose is plugged, and he is holding a banner that reads, "ALL LIVES MATTER!

WizdomTalk was, unexpectedly, present at the cartel's gathering. He had sat in Colonel Kligoff's empty chair, quietly listening. He had remained invisible to everyone in the room. WizdomTalk was underestimated by Dark Shadows and the Babylonian Cartel.

Wizdomtalk The Dreammaker

PORT OF HAMAD - QATAR

The following week, the Saker Falcons soar high above the Port of Hamad in Qatar unchallenged. People rush to catch transit to their various destinations as giant oil tankers pass in a magnificent parade. A handsome character appears out of nowhere, dressed in a rumpled black tuxedo with a white ruffled shirt, large purple sneakers on his feet, and a speckled Middle Eastern scarf. Yes, WizdomTalk is a remarkable sight!

He completes his look with a black baseball cap and gold-rimmed sunglasses on the bridge of his nose. Regardless of his unusual attire, his peppermint aroma charmed everyone in his vicinity.

WizdomTalk arrived at the seaport, looking for a ship bound for the Mariana Islands. He is on a quest to convey a message that will affect the entire world. He discovered two boats, *The Safe Passage,* and *The Unsafe Passage,* when he arrived.

He noticed a magnificent luxury ship arriving in the distance; he approached *The Safe Passage* and asked for a ride. The islands were too far away, and the Marianas Trench was too deep and perilous to cross, according to the ship's captain. As a result, WizdomTalk approached the ship of the *Unsafe Passage*. Captain Tricky, the ship's owner, kept a ravenous Tiger Shark as a pet. He was using a bone to sharpen its teeth.

When Captain Tricky sees WizdomTalk, he assumes he is an idiot because he is dressed so outrageously. The shark smiles cunningly as he salivates at the prospect of consuming WizdomTalk for lunch. WizdomTalk accepts the captain's offer to bring him to the Mariana Islands. WizdomTalk, pretending to be naive, accepts the captain's offer with joy.

"Does your ship offer first-class accommodations?" he asks the skipper, smiling. "Yes, we do," the astute Captain Tricky exclaimed, "and we will provide you as a lovely free lunch!"

"Great!" WizdomTalk responded by saying, "I've never taken a ship in first class before. What kind of lodging will I have?"

"Of course, my friend, it will be in the belly of the shark," the skipper remarked with a devious smile. The captain puts his hand over his lips and apologizes. "Oh, sorry," he adds, "I meant to say the ship's belly, where the greatest accommodations are." "Umm, thank you for your generous offer," WizdomTalk stammers, "but I'll take another vessel today."

"What is the ship's name, Sir?" Captain Tricky says, smirking. WizdomTalk responds, "THE KILLER WHALE!" The captain screams,

"Respectfully, Sir. It has the potential to consume you!" He jokingly inquired, "Are you insane?"

WizdomTalk said with a huge grin on his face, "Of course, I am a little insane like a crafty fox! That is something you did not know?" As soon as he turned his back, the cunning Tiger Shark was intending to eat WizdomTalk for lunch.

"OK, maybe we'll travel together another time?" Captain Tricky says quickly.

Finally, The Killer Whale, a massive luxury vessel, arrived at the Port of Hamad. WizdomTalk walked along the pier, with his back to the captain. The Tiger Shark slowly approaches WizdomTalk, drooling and waiting to consume his "dumb" prey in the water beside the dock. The shark, however, was blind to the fishermen putting a net behind him, which miraculously grabbed the Tiger Shark in mid-flight.

WizdomTalk smiles and turns around to wave goodbye to the shark, yelling, "HEY, DON'T FORGET, NO SUCH THING AS A FREE LUNCH EXISTS!"

The once-dominant Tiger Shark was on the verge of extinction and appealed for rescue with its eyes. WizdomTalk felt sympathy for the shark as he gazed out across the gulf. As a result, he wiggles his brows and points his fingers at the fishing net, which miraculously breaks and releases the shark.

As the Tiger Shark dove deeper into the gulf, he pondered: "Sir, I owe you a huge debt of gratitude! I am thinking of becoming a vegetarian!" He instantly heard the answer to his thoughts roaring from across the waves, as he wondered why and how this strange man had set him free.

"I set you free to teach you a lesson, my friend. Never judge a book by its cover; rather, judge it by its content! You should not judge a person solely based on their appearance or manner but based on their character and conduct. When it comes to deception and manipulation, you must be extremely cautious since there is always someone sharper and craftier than you.

Keep in mind that the person you are attempting to harm could one day save your life. I wield a powerful force known as "WIZDOMPOWER!!!" Anyone, including you, may learn to use this power", WizdomTalk said. He boarded the enormous luxury ship after completing his lecture to this crazy shark. WizdomTalk sat on the ship's deck, drinking a frosty drink, in the cool breeze.

He considers spreading WIZDOMPOWER's concepts, tools, and life lessons across the world as he reflects on his most recent experience. He reflected on his intended destination, the Mariana Islands. He also considers the Babylonian Cartel's global intentions for the destruction of humanity, particularly the youth.

The Sage is looking forward to speaking at the World Youth Summit 20/25 with optimism. His mind drifts as he settles deeper into a peaceful mood. He recalls meeting his protégé, Major General Bain, and his underperforming commandos on the desert battleground known as *Sumer*.

Unleash Your Vision

SUMER, THE BEGINNING

TAT! TAT! TAT! POW! POW! POW!

The Sage begins to dream as the ship's vibrations rock him to sleep. Without warning, bursting Scud and Patriot missiles light up the skies over ancient Sumer, now known as Iraq. These were commonplace in October 1990 in Iraq during the first Gulf War. Beautiful hanging gardens previously graced this site. The area is now being ravaged by war.

Sumer, also known as Mesopotamia or Babylon in ancient times, was one of the world's oldest civilizations. Sumer, which is now southern Iraq, means "the land of the civilized kings."

For ages, researchers have been drawn to and enthralled by this great culture's achievements and elite society. On the Persian Gulf coast, the Sumerian metropolis of Eridu was one of the world's first modern towns, brimming with affluence, knowledge, and potential.

Now, as Allied Forces and Iraq's Republican Guard soldiers fight in vicious, non-stop warfare, lethal rockets sizzle through the air. Homes, schools, and hospitals are being reduced to ruins, riddled with gunshots, and ravaged by smoke and fire.

The entire country is terrified, as they witness their towns being pillaged and destroyed. The people are filled with anguish and despair. Innocent families seek refuge and make desperate pleas. The tragic reality of war is that innocent people always pay the highest price in terms of loss of life, liberty, and property.

Dark poisonous smoke, anguish, terror, and death leave a trail of trauma that will continue for generations. There is, however, a strange chest with the ability to alter negative thoughts and behaviors. It is a massive power that will prove to be a source of illumination, bringing humanity peace and prosperity.

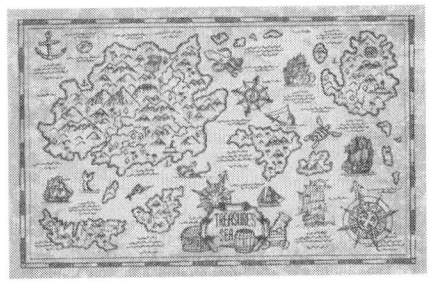

THE ANTIQUITIES MISSION

Bain, the Major General, is a tall, blond-haired Australian with a commanding presence. He works for the United Nations Antiquities Unit as a Special Forces Officer. Other than scorched skin from years under the hot desert sun, he has few identifying features.

The General fantasizes of swimming with dolphins in his homeland's calm blue waters. However, there was no opportunity to swim with dolphins in this location. Amid a violent war, he commands a troop of soldiers and scholars in the sweltering desert.

The General was fortunate in that this was his final deployment before retiring the next month. Then, at his leisure, he intends to open a hotel with his money and retirement benefits

The General's new mission is to oversee a team of "battle competent" commandos who serve member states of the United Nations (U.N).

What these commandos did not realize was that their countries had loaned them to the U.N. Antiquities team. They were seen as throwaway misfits and underachievers by their governments.

Their supervisors believe it would be difficult for them to mess up such a straightforward operation. Who cared about antiquities in the first place?

Except for the commandos' General, none of these combatants had held an elevated position in the military but had proven their worth in warfare. Even though several of them had university degrees, they had only risen to the ranks of Corporal and Sergeant.

Because of their poor conduct and personal decisions, these troops were skipped over for advancements. Everything the troops do is influenced by their bad attitudes.

The Antiquities commandos take a break in the shade of a pomegranate tree during the midday heat. Scotty, a corporal from the Bayou of Louisiana in North America, was one of them, and he was sitting, mocking a gigantic viper snake.

He is an avid athlete at home and enjoys wrestling alligators in his spare time. Scotty's ambition in life is to win an Olympic gold medal in wrestling. The viper snake grows tired of his mocking and bites him without notice! Scotty begins to panic and convulse almost immediately.

Ebony, the medic, was a tall, shapely Caribbean woman with short dreadlocks. She likes to sing and play the steel drums and wanted to be a medical doctor. Her life's ambition is to treat the impoverished. She, unfortunately, is afflicted with low self-esteem.

Nasim, a village sheepherder, was dancing and playing reggae music on the steel drum with Ebony. They came to a halt when they noticed a ruckus and heard Corporal Scotty yell. Ebony accidentally trips over the drum and gets knocked out! Scotty cries, "Help!"

Nasim is enthralled by the eccentric foreigner's backward antics! He hits Scotty in the face while laughing uncontrollably and calling him an idiot in Arabic. He informs Scotty that the snake was not dangerous and that all his symptoms were caused by his imagination. Those present laugh at Scotty, as Nasim continues to call him an idiot in Arabic.

"Attention!!!" cries one of the other soldiers as Major General Bain drives his army jeep into the village compound.

Wizdomtalk The Dreammaker

UNDERACHIEVERS

When the General and his civilian assistant arrived at the settlement, the sun had risen to its maximum point. While the soldiers are standing at attention, Major General Bain addresses them. He then goes into the details of the covert operation. The General is a likeable character who is curious about the lives and goals of his troops. Each soldier took a turn identifying himself and explaining why they were in their current situation.

Ali is a Middle Easterner with a background in military planning, being a falconer is his favorite hobby. He wears a falcon on his shoulders because of this. Ali's ambitions in life were straightforward, he wanted to work for the government, start a family, and be a decent husband and father.

Unleash Your Vision

Corporal Zing is a native of Asia with a passion for technology and basketball. His one and only ambition was to create ground-breaking technology that would transform the planet. After that, there was Africa's Corporal Chika. He overcame learning problems as a child and now aspires to be a prominent university's literary professor.

Corporal Renaldo is from South America and is a married father. He aspires to be a professional soccer coach but does not be available to practice.

Sergeant Wellington, a European, desired to find cures for ailments. Corporal Rebecca is a stunning young woman from the Caucasus Mountains who can sing like an angel.

Corporal Mario, a Central American excavator, his ambition is to amass a substantial sum of money. Sukioma, a Pacific Islander, rounds off the group of warring men and women. He is shy and lacks the bravery to speak in public, despite being a chaplain.

The soldiers switch their attention to a group of villagers after learning about the General and his troops.

THE BEDOUINS

Carlos, an American volunteer teacher, was standing close to the commandos. He tutored a small group of students at a local school. When the soldiers watched him engage with the kids, he came off as friendly and amusing, despite being a little overweight.

Salem and Hadeeth, two of his students, were pre-teen village girls who were both clever and shy. Abu, a 14-year-old rugged-looking youth, sat calmly beneath a fig tree. They enjoyed living in the village even though it had no electricity, plumbing, or internet. Not being used to having many visitors the foreign soldiers extremely enthralled the youth.

Except for occasional sad news from Bedouin caravans, the small village remains undisturbed by the Iraqi conflict. The youngsters in the community have no access to contemporary technology. Picking figs, working in the market, or herding sheep and goats, as their ancestors did for millennia, are all part of their daily routine.

The General started to make the teacher a suspect. Even though he believed his suspicions were correct, he chose not to tell the teacher or the rest of the team. So, for the time being, he chooses to leave the teacher alone. He was, however, not far off, as Carlos, the teacher, was an American intelligence agent on an undercover mission in Iraq.

He was not the sweet and innocent person he pretended to be. He had a high IQ, was multilingual, and had been schooled in espionage and military tactics.

He was recruited from a university. A spy agency provided him with training. His missions took him all over the world, and he worked in covert operations.

Carlos pretended to be a teacher, a low-level embassy employee, a humanitarian worker, or a paramilitary soldier as part of his cover story. Carlos' spy missions cost him his spouse, home, children, good friends, spirituality, and sanity. Fortunately, this was his final duty, and he is now quietly helping General Bain's United Nations effort.

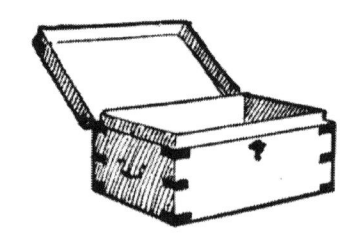

PEPPERMINT CHEST

The commandos had unearthed important antique artifacts earlier in the week in a local goat herding community. A spectacular treasure box brimming with gold and white diamonds was one of the relics discovered. It had an inscription on it that was weird and unfamiliar. The commandos were astounded to smell peppermint and hear delicate Middle Eastern drumming emanating from this strange chest.

Their finding, on the other hand, had an immediate and undeniable effect on their actions. These tough troops became confused, powerless, and shook in their boots from fright when they were exposed to this chest for some unexplained reason.

A U.N. team of highly qualified archaeologists, linguists, and historians comes in a Black Hawk helicopter. Colonel Boris Kligoff oversees escorting the U.N. delegation out of Russia. He is a huge, loud Russian soldier with a commanding presence who prefers Cuban cigars.

The purpose of the U.N. team is to save historical objects in museums throughout the world so that future generations can learn from them. The present objective is to collect, identify, and decipher the codes found on all ancient Sumerian artifacts.

The mission of the commando is to keep this exclusive gathering of academics safe. The scholars looked at the chest and were terrified and astonished as well. Just as the treasure chest started to vibrate, they heard beautiful Middle Eastern drumming.

Professor Notsobright of Heidelberg University in Germany is a well-known ancient linguist. He declares that the chest's inscription reads, "WIZDOMTALK: The DREAMMAKER" in an ancient tongue after hours of research.

Despite their fear, the scholars felt they had no choice but to open the chest and see what was inside. They carefully open the chest and find an antique papyrus manuscript inside. The air surrounding them is immediately filled with a peppermint-scented mist.

This extraordinary mist seizes and draws all the villagers, soldiers, and scholars into the chest one by one. Nobody had time to contemplate or be concerned since it happened so quickly.

As dazzling colorful lights raced around them, the group plunged into a vast tunnel. Their minds became as teenagers in an instant, but some adult characteristics were still present. They all abruptly stopped moving when they heard a loud thump. Then came a long pause!

They touched down near a tent on a gorgeous and green seaside oasis.

Freshwater and fruit can be found in abundance. They detected the scent of sweet peppermint in the air and heard a funky musical beat but were unable to locate its source.

They seized their weapons for a fight, stunned by their young transformation, but the firearms melted like butter. Then they all heard a gentle voice say, "Thank you for stopping by.

Still invisible, WizdomTalk offered them a meal and a place to rest. "WizdomTalk is my name. I am a DREAMMAKER, as well as a Noble Patriarch and a Master Sage." The Professor is approached by his voice that roars with laughter, revealing only footprints on the sand and nothing else.

The Sage declared, "I gave you all young, receptive brains so you may learn to be DREAMMAKERS and ACHIEVERS in more areas of your lives. When it comes to learning, adults can be lazy, stubborn, and set in their ways."

Unleash Your Vision

The group became exhausted at that point. "The Noble Patriarchs will be discussed the next day," said WizdomTalk. They slept at that point, unsure of who this WIZDOMTALK was.

The perfume of peppermint fills the air the next day. The now-young group was overjoyed to discover a table brimming with refreshing and tasty fruits and vegetables.

"Do not be concerned! Consume! You have a long way to go. Let us walk along the Oasis," remarked invisible WizdomTalk after everyone had eaten. Everyone thought to themselves, "Who is this voice directing us around?" WizdomTalk, however, was still invisible, so no one could strike.

Then, quickly, a smiling, young-looking, and oddly clad figure of a guy emerges from a cloud of smoke. He had kind eyes and a contagious smile, which quickly boosted the Oasis' atmosphere. "An old camel is smarter than a young goat most of the time!" WizdomTalk said.

Because they did not grasp his logic, the warriors and scholars were uninterested.

Even yet, the villagers listened intently and grasped the meaning of the adage. Because of their wisdom, most elderly individuals are smarter than young people, according to the saying.

According to WizdomTalk, "You invited me, an old camel, into your existence when you young goats unlocked the antique chest. You must now learn about knowledge and how to unleash your vision and strength to live more successful and productive lives. You may even find that you are happier and have more pleasant experiences in your life."

He continues, "The Noble Patriarchs and Matriarchs, who are my friends, are knowledgeable ancestors or seniors who seem like ancient camels. They are a unique breed of people whose job is to safeguard and preserve the family or community. Love, generosity, encouragement, fairness, integrity, and strength are among the virtues they uphold and follow.

They are priceless and their wisdom exceeds that of any ocean. They can be found in any country on the planet. Their careers could range from farming to being heads of state. Since the beginning of time, their wisdom has been the backbone of humanity. The wisdom and respect of these Noble Patriarchs and Matriarchs are a missing link in today's world. Wisdom is their defining quality. They comprehend the world in which they live, complete with its paradoxes and deceptions.

You may have a title or a skill, but you lack the ability to determine your own fate," WizdomTalk finished.

The soldiers rushed WizdomTalk after his lecture, tying his hands and feet. "We've got you now, crazy man! We are in control now!" The General exclaimed in a childish tone. "I just told you young goats that an old camel is usually smarter than a young goat!" WizdomTalk said.

The troops mocking WizdomTalk made the villagers sad. The General attempts but fails to slap the Sage.

"If you want to go home, it's in that direction," WizdomTalk reminded the troops and scholars, pointing up in the air.

WizdomTalk smiled as he freed himself and talked to the village youngsters and residents, saying, "Let us go for a walk along the beach and leave the goats to their own devices. We'll eat a delicious meal while learning about Dark Shadows."

The troops and academics looked across at The General with remorse, regretting their judgment and disdain for WizdomTalk. They were all silently pondering the subject, "What is Dark Shadows?"

Wizdomtalk The Dreammaker

THE DARK SHADOWS

As they travel along the fresh oasis, a big white dove floats above the troops, scholars, and village inhabitants. They start to notice a foul odor of sulfur wafting in their direction. Everyone was holding their noses and wondering where this foul odor was coming from.

"Warning, look!" Dark Shadows is hiding behind the fig trees, attempting to blend in, but unfortunately for him, a foul odor of sulfur follows him wherever he goes. "Hey, Dark Shadows, you buzzard, I can see you!" exclaims WizdomTalk.

Surprisingly, a white dove appeared in the sky and warned the gathering, saying, "Beware, know your enemy!"

Unleash Your Vision

Continuing to teach, Wizdomtalk shares "Dark Shadows signifies any bad, negative, or detrimental element in your life that is threatening your happiness.

But keep in mind that a challenge can occasionally solve a problem. When your opponent challenges the basis of your position, for example, in a debate, it allows you to evaluate, defend, and argue your point of view.

It would allow you to express yourself freely while also allowing you to develop intellectually. When someone tries to push or deceive you into embracing their point of view, that is a negative challenge. Dark Shadows comes with negative challenges.

Dark Shadows also poses a serious and dangerous hazard to your health. Dark Shadows wants you to adopt his pessimistic outlook on life, which will stifle your ability to dream and plan. He comes at you with military precision and deliberateness.

The Dark Shadow begins by attacking your mind, sowing doubt, and uncertainty. He is attempting to ruin your positive and productive attitude on life by whatever means necessary, leaving you in despair.

Since the dawn of time, Dark Shadows has been present. Dark Shadows' victims are buried in graveyards all throughout the world, never realizing their full potential because of his poisonous pessimism. What a waste of potential, wealth, and possibilities in life. Their abilities may have been put to better use and for the better!

Dark Shadows creates a skewed image to lower or build your self-worth and self-esteem. Dark Shadows is out to steal your ambition or control your vision and creativity. If someone had the vision to build a profitable business, he may attack, instilling self-doubt in others who engaged in the idea. He is happiest when you and everyone around you, despite your abilities, question your potential and capabilities.

The Dark Shadows want to denigrate you as a valuable person, despite your deepest insight. He will suffocate your dreams, suffocate your self-esteem, and suffocate your pleasure.

Fortunately, Dark Shadows can be stopped and destroyed by four opposing superpowers. Truth, Wisdom, Courage, and Faith are all opponents of negativity! You'll learn about Arrested Development tomorrow."

ARRESTED DEVELOPMENT

The pouring rain was pleasant in the scorching desert. A cover was fashioned out of palm leaves by the village residents. The group came upon two date trees on their walk. One tree is completely matured, while the growth of the other appears to be stunted. "Why do some trees never reach their full potential?" a soldier inquires of the Sage.

"You know, personal growth can be like these trees," WizdomTalk said. "We all have goals of what we want to accomplish when we grow up as gifted youngsters. Consider a youngster who aspires to be a professional tennis player.

They begin with considerable zeal and lofty expectations of realizing their dreams.

Anyone who wants to achieve wonderful things in life or in their industry must first grasp the fundamentals. They will only improve their performance through trial and error and practice.

They are, nevertheless, deemed professionals if they have achieved that higher degree via study and effort. Years of dedication may be required. This method can be used to attain any goal, whether it is related to work, hobbies, a profession, or even important relationships. Any worthy activity can benefit from this development process.

Dark Shadows, unfortunately, is a negative energy that frequently leaves trauma and stress in its wake. People's tremendous potential is robbed, and their ability to dream is crushed, because of the consequence. Most people have forgotten their true power because of the trauma they have been through because of physical, mental, or emotional abuse.

Obstacles can make it difficult for us to recall who we "REALLY" are. Trauma and obstacles occur in a variety of kinds and sizes. Physical disabilities, the death of a loved one, sexual, physical, and emotional abuse, debt, divorce, and abandonment are all examples of life events that can have a negative impact on a child's development.

Traumatic events, especially when they occur when we are young, have an impact on our mental and emotional development, as well as our intellectual performance and general view on life.

Dark Shadows is a supernatural entity that can see through to your actual potential. His primary focus is on those people with the most potential to achieve extraordinary things in life. Dark Shadows understands that if he can weaken someone while they are still young and stop their development, they will not reach their full potential.

They will give up! They will stop dreaming, lose hope, and give up on their dreams and ambitions! Many talented people are held in prisons and mental hospitals because their development was stifled during their childhood. They may aspire to be nice people who make a meaningful contribution to society.

These people are unable to move on from their past experiences and the sorrow and suffering that comes with it. They frequently repeat unpleasant prior habits in the hopes of achieving a different outcome. This is the epitome of insane behavior! You may appear to be managing your life well on the outside, but your life may be in chaos on the inside.

If you believe you have experienced trauma that is preventing you from moving ahead in a healthy way, please know that getting professional treatment is perfectly acceptable.

It is the right thing to do, and it is never too late to start! It is a matter of life and death! Let us talk about Wisdom now."

Unleash Your Vision

WISDOM

The sky and beach were bleak and gloomy the next day when WizdomTalk met the troops, scholars, and village residents. "Are you ready to journey to a place of higher learning?" The Sage inquires. With a little look of trepidation, the group stared at him.

"Where are we going?" Corporal Chika inquires. "Intelligence University!" exclaims the Sage. As he guides them to a parked long green scooter. They all climb in and are whisked away to a vast, sunlit campus bustling with life.

The campus youth were preoccupied with gaining knowledge, learning, and achieving success.

They soon come upon a bald owl with glasses and a fantastic smile. He is introduced to the group as Owl, the

Professor, by WizdomTalk. The fact that Owl could communicate astounded the group. Owl encourages them to have a seat on the grassy slope and make themselves at home.

Professor Owl starts the day's lesson by declaring, "It makes no difference how old you are or how many mistakes you have made in your life. Learning, knowledge, and wisdom are the only things that can turn time and failures into success. When someone has wisdom, they have knowledge that goes well beyond their brain.

We can effectively engage our intellect, apply solid judgment, and take appropriate action in our daily lives if we have wisdom. We can also learn from other sources like books, professors, and other people's experiences. A person who ignores his or her inner wisdom is prone to folly and idiocy. There is something far more important than education and information, and that is WISDOM.

We all can expose this inner wisdom through the growing of our minds, bodies, and souls. It is so deep that you may not even be aware of its presence until you require it. Wisdom, however, is constantly present, and ready to assist you.

Consider the case of a well-educated individual seeking a path to success. They arrive at a fork in the road where the path splits three ways.

Road A is unpaved, dirty, and bumpy. *Road B* is a hilly, rocky road. *Road C* is brand new, smooth, and level."

They do not ask a haggard and elderly woman named, Wisdom dozing under a tree at the fork in the road for directions since she is haggard and elderly. The Seeker would most certainly pick *Road C* because it is smooth and newly paved, relying solely on their intellect and knowledge.

Wisdom, on the other hand, would lead him to take Road A." A young girl's brow furrowed in concentration. "She wondered why this Seeker would choose to travel on an unpaved road when he could travel on a smooth route?"

With a smile on his face, the Professor says, "We are only able to see what is immediately in front of us because of our intellect. We are oblivious to the fact that *Road C* is paved for only a short distance and leads to a stinky rubbish dump.

Furthermore, despite her looks, we cannot deduce that the old woman resting under the tree is unknowledgeable. She knew the town of "SUCCESS" was only a little distance beyond the uneven road.

Because they never bothered to wake Wisdom up to ask for directions, many clever individuals missed the route to prosperity. As the Seeker, they rely solely on their intellect to avoid feeling uncomfortable on the "difficult" path and they fail to seek counsel on the most effective way to achievement.

Our decisions are obvious at times. When making significant decisions, however, we must learn to use both wisdom and knowledge. Otherwise, you can end up in the DUMP like this Seeker!

Keep in mind to embrace wisdom, and it will gladly accept you. There are obstacles on the way to success. You must, for example, learn to resist Dark Shadows. Tomorrow, you will start to uncover who you are as a winner, including your originality, vision, power, and great gifts," said Owl, Professor.

Owl, the Professor, graciously shook everyone's hand before leading the group back to the green scooter. They all exchanged a smile and said, "Professor, thank you so much. We hope to see you again soon!" The scooter then sped away.

Unleash Your Vision

Respect Life

YOU WERE BORN A WINNER

After a relaxing afternoon and having a delicious lunch, the Sage took a little nap. WizdomTalk then started telling a narrative. WizdomTalk began his lesson by saying, "Today, I hope to demonstrate to you that the Most-High who is the Creator is without error.

The rustic Champion Volcano began to rumble one Saturday night in the town of Winners, as if it were going to give birth!" Soft drumming could be heard as WizdomTalk wiggled his dimples.

Then, for some reason, everyone vanished, and he brought them back in time to *Winner's Hospital.*

WizdomTalk continues to speak, "A team of doctors and nurses in blue and white uniforms waited patiently in the delivery ward to help guide and watch the birth of something special, a baby!

You are misguided if you believe your appearance on this planet is by chance. I will show you that you have come to accomplish a specific goal that only you can achieve. You are a one-of-a-kind, irreplaceable human on a mission.

Science can verify or disprove a wide range of theories. Science can also back up truths. To prove your uniqueness, I am going to use science to prove that you were born a winner with limitless power!

Whatever the circumstances of your birth may appear to be, you were not born by chance. Because you were triumphant, when your life began! Up to ten million sperms are discharged during human mating. The fight to live and properly create life must then begin for each sperm cell.

Imagine being up against such a formidable foe! Your first interaction with the forces of Dark Shadows occurred during your conception. You, on the other hand, outmaneuvered 9,999,999 opponents like a pro soccer player!

You, the survivor, were the only sperm that was allowed to participate in the fertilization process. You battled bacteria and viruses while you grew in the womb, and they were a constant threat to your survival. But you were born nine months later, on a bright sunny day, with much acclaim.

You made your existence known with a courteous cry, a smile, or a scream as you took your first breath. If you are reading this, it means you are not only a survivor, but also a victor! Let us talk about Purpose now!"

YOU HAVE A PURPOSE

WizdomTalk greets the Middle Eastern youngsters with a grin and an embrace, then asks them, "What is your reason for living?"

"We don't know," the naive children responded, staring deeply into the Sage's eyes. "Let's have some fun!" remarked the Sage.

WizdomTalk wrinkles his nose and tilts his head to the right, pointing down, while soft drumming begins. A kite appears out of nowhere! The Sage tells the kids to hold their breath and clutch the kite's string.

The party is mysteriously taken deep beneath the water before arriving at a toy factory in Singapore. Even though no one gets wet, all this activity takes place!

The building is crammed with bright, fun toys and gadgets. The cheerful kids are overjoyed to be there with so much activity.

WizdomTalk said, "When a creator creates something, it is for their own benefit, not for the benefit of the created. When artisans decide to produce a toy, for example, they must first decide the purpose for which the device will be used, for the blueprint to be suitable for that use.

Let us say they determine the toy's aim is to convey delight to children while teaching them math. The Creator is meticulous in following the design's every detail and never deviates from the blueprint. When the toy is finished, the inventor sells it to the public. Parents purchase the toy to help their children learn math.

Others are content simply having the toy in their possession! One woman might notice the toy and decide to purchase it as a decorative item. Someone else may obtain the toy but never use it. Some people may buy the toy with the intention of using it for something different than that for which it was designed.

The toy's original goal, on the other hand, has not changed. In your life, the same idea applies. Nothing can change the reality that we were all created for a certain purpose by our Creator. If you look around, you will notice that people serve a variety of purposes. Some people work as healers, while others work as educators; others construct, entertain, govern, or investigate.

You may already be aware of some components of your life's mission. Your purpose is not a secret. To find it, you often must look deep within yourself. On your path to success, defining your mission will be a significant element of your life's work. You need to learn to be a DREAMMAKER."

He continued by saying, "Don't worry if you don't know what your ultimate mission is right now; you will one day. Keep in mind that accidents are unavoidable. You were created with a plan and a purpose from the moment you were conceived in the womb. Let us take a closer look at how you're a Masterpiece of art now."

Unleash Your Vision

YOU ARE A WORK OF ART

When WizdomTalk agreed to meet the children by the coast, it was a very calm day. He passed around unusual-looking seashells he found in his treasure basket. "These are the first shells I've ever seen; they have an unusual appearance." Yazmin exclaimed.

WizdomTalk starts to yawn and mysteriously summons a purple pillow, on which he falls asleep. He started snoring loudly just where he was standing! The children burst out laughing at his wild antics. The Sage awoke minutes later and started his instruction and spoke as if nothing had happened.

"Each of these shells is a work of art, just like you! Everyone is made to be a masterpiece. A masterpiece is a piece of art that is extremely rare and precious. Only one of you was created by the Creator. You are unique and special in the sense that no one else is precisely like you and that each of your lives has an important purpose.

You are a magnificent gift to the world.

Mountains of gold are not worth as much as you are. The world is waiting for you to manifest good things, my friends. It is your job to identify and live your destiny. Do not delude yourselves into believing otherwise," the Sage stated.

The group began to understand their worth and significance in the world, and they asked, "What is this Power I wield?"

Unleash Your Vision

YOU HAVE POWER!

The warriors, villagers, and intellectuals relaxed the next evening after delicious food and music, then WizdomTalk came. He wiggles his eyebrows and clicks his fingers, accompanied by subtle drumming, and butterfly lights begin to flood the desert. "I turned on the lights to show you the horrible Dark Shadows who lurked amid the woods. This character will constantly stand in opposition to what I teach you," WizdomTalk opined.

The village kids started putting their hands over their noses to block out his foul odor. They pursued Dark Shadows into the sea, knowing very well that he would return.

"Let's go on," WizdomTalk says. "Consider how much power you have! You can reason. You are imaginative and compassionate. You can make decisions because you have the willpower to do so. You can think quicker and more efficiently than any machine ever made, even if you only use 10% of your brain. You have an untapped talent in the 90% of your brain that you do not even use.

Humans have dominion over all living things on the planet. People have harnessed the power of the air to go to the moon. Humans have both made peace and created war. Through the power of belief, faith, and action, you can achieve everything your mind can imagine.

Scientists have lately been able to clone human beings, their organs, and animals in laboratories using deoxyribonucleic acid (DNA). Although these clones may resemble and match our species' physical characteristics, they fail to accurately express our personalities and spirits.

I believe we should study the power of Words."

Unleash Your Vision

THE POWER OF YOUR WORDS

When one of the scholars inquired about transporting them to the Brazilian Rainforest, WizdomTalk said, "Yes, please allow us to go in style. Welcome to the magical carpet!"

When they arrive, they are greeted by a swarm of brightly colored talking skunks surrounded by luxuriant flora. To the other skunk, one negative skunk yelled, "Get away from me! You are filthy and you stink!"

"Yes, I smell—very sweet and wonderful!" exclaims the other positive skunk as he laughs and shouts aloud. The skunks' remarks to the islanders were too funny as they double over laughing.

Wizdomtalk The Dreammaker

The positive skunk said, "Allowing others to put you down is not acceptable. Low self-esteem will prevent you from reaching your objectives. Seeds of high self-esteem have been sown in you! For you to grow and flourish, these seeds must be tended and nurtured.

Your beliefs can develop and generate, much like seeds. Your belief system is like a plant that needs to be nurtured and maintained through positive self-talk. Others will not believe and think well of you if you do not believe and think well of yourself. Others may feel better about themselves if you feel good about yourself.

Make a commitment to refrain from negative self-talk. Be aware that even crickets can use negative self-talk to convince themselves to be silent. Your words and actions have a lot of impact. As a result, you should always think before speaking!

Your imagination is powerful and can send messages in the form of thoughts, which can then be translated into words, and those words can then be translated into behaviors.

Words have incredible power! Words are sharper than a sword, and they can pierce others' hearts faster than a bullet.

Build and employ pleasant, enlightening, and encouraging terms in your vocabulary. If possible, speak positively about others, avoid gossip and lying, and live a peaceful existence.

Unleash Your Vision

Always give encouraging words to children and individuals with mental problems and avoid putting down or labeling others.

Never tell a youngster or a person with a mental or physical disability that they are condemned to fail in life. Who are we to pass judgement? We have no idea what the future holds!" the positive skunk finished speaking.

"Let's study about your image," WizdomTalk stated after thanking the skunks and unplugging his nose to breathe the sweet smell.

YOU DEFINE YOUR IMAGE

WizdomTalk brought the group to another cool oasis in the desert today. They discovered a massive mirror there.

The Mirror is introduced to them by the Sage. The Mirror began to speak, much to the children's surprise, and asked, "What do you see when you look at yourself in the mirror?

Is the image in the mirror, an accurate or distorted reflection of who you are? How do you feel about the way you look?" WizdomTalk began to yawn unexpectedly as

The Mirror talked. Then the Sage smiled and, by pointing at the rest of the group, he managed to put them all to sleep. After 30 minutes, they all awoke, and the Mirror completes its lesson without missing a beat.

The Mirror asks the people: "Have you ever been told you're unattractive? Have you ever been told that you will not be able to reach your goals? Have you ever been told that you are not smart enough to achieve your objectives?

Has anyone ever made you feel that you would not be able to achieve your life goals because of your ethnicity, skin color, disability, or family background? Have you ever told yourself that you are not clever enough, handsome enough, or skilled enough? Do you think you are inadequate when you compare yourself to others?

Do you believe you are overweight or underweight? Do you ever wonder where these recommendations and ideas come from? The messages we receive from influences outside of ourselves can often shape our perceptions of ourselves. These concepts are frequently derived from social media, novels, movies, music lyrics, online videos, radio, and television.

They also come from those we know well, such as our parents, friends, peers, and teachers. What you think about yourself is also influenced by your culture, religion, and the community in which you live.

Because the visuals in the media may not be real, your view of others may also be skewed.

People on television and in magazines, for example, may appear more handsome, taller, slender, prettier, smarter, healthier, and wealthier than they really are.

They hire 'image-makers,' whose duty it is to use cosmetics, haircuts, and clothing to make movie stars, politicians, athletes, leaders, and notable people seem fantastic. Photographs of celebrities and notable people are airbrushed to give them a pristine image.

Have you ever wondered what it is like to meet renowned individuals in person? They are folks who are like you. When you compare yourself to others, you will constantly fall short and never be satisfied.

To put it another way, if you believe you must dress or look a certain way to be accepted, you will lose sight of the fact that you are a one-of-a-kind masterpiece.

You must guard your mind against negative self-talk with zeal. Every day, remind yourself that you are unique and cherish the things that make you exceptional.

Remember that artists, like you, create images. Tomorrow, you will learn about your Gifts!" the Mirror stated as it fell silent.

YOU ARE EXTRAORDINARILY GIFTED

"How would you like to go to the Wimbledon Tennis Tournament in London, England?" WizdomTalk asks the group on a bright and beautiful day.

The Sage wiggles his eyebrows and points east, where a large basket looms on the horizon. The troops, scholars, and village residents could not contain their joy. The bucket started spinning once everyone was on board. The group was at a Wimbledon tennis tournament in minutes, observing world-class athletes.

WizdomTalk began teaching with his finest British accent. "Let us talk about your gifts and talents now that you've realized your power and individuality. You do not have the same gifts as everyone else. They may resemble each other, but they are not identical.

Allow me to explain the distinction between gifts and abilities. We are all born with one-of-a-kind and uncommon abilities. Through learning and practice, we may hone specialized skills, thanks to our unique abilities.

Musicians, for example, have received formal training at music schools all around the world. They were taught by the top teachers in the world. Many have spent years studying and practicing mastering their craft.

'Child prodigies' are born with exceptionally elevated levels of intelligence and abilities. Prodigies can be found in any field. These kids excel not only in music but also in science, sports, and technology. It may appear unnatural or impossible for these children to have such advanced skills at an early age.

Despite their special capabilities, they continue to study and practice to bring their abilities to the surface. We must practice our gifts, just like a prodigy, to keep and express them, identifying and utilizing our abilities aids in the development of strong self-esteem, confidence, and recognition of our true worth.

The Creator has a big plan in store for you! It is about you and how you can make a positive difference in your family, friends, and the world around you! You are a powerful drop of water with the same abilities and endowments as the cosmic ocean.

Unleash Your Vision

There is nothing you cannot accomplish or achieve if you believe this. When others try to put you down, or when you start to put yourself down with negative self-talk and doubt, remember who you are. You are a priceless gem brimming with awe and bravery! Tomorrow, in the afternoon, we'll discuss Societal Roles."

SOCIETY'S LEADERSHIP ROLES

It was the middle of the day, and the sun was blistering! While pondering, Sergeant Wellington walked into sand full of enormous red ants. As the ants began to attack him, he bounced up and down on one leg, screaming.

Ebony, the combat-ready medic, sprang into action and began treating his injuries. While the Sergeant received medical attention, everyone else waited.

WizdomTalk raised his hand, and a blue marble bathtub appeared from the skies. "What is he doing?" exclaimed the crowd. "Is he going to undress and take a bath right in front of us?!" they cried.

Unleash Your Vision

But, once again, the Sage fooled them by climbing into the empty but inviting tub and falling asleep quickly.

WizdomTalk awoke an hour later, rejuvenated, to continue his lecture and spoke. "Isn't it true that many of you here aspire to be successful leaders? But there is a catch: you do not know how! Today, I will show you how to use something called WIZDOMPOWER to get what you want!!!

Take a good look at this ant colony. It is an excellent example of how effective leadership is critical to the development of a prosperous society. When you look attentively, you will notice that every ant is hard at work.

Others are gathering resources for the colony's construction, while others are transporting food. Some ants are supervising over other ants. As you can see, they each have a distinct function. All colonies have a Queen Ant, which is their leader.

Someone who can control, manage, and guide people is referred to as a leader. Every ant colony, like our human society, needs a leader. A leader can direct others toward achieving a common goal or a specialized task.

No matter how old you are, you may be a bad or good leader, however, the first leadership role one must assume is to lead oneself based on the decisions one makes.

The quality of your life will be determined by the decisions you make. What if you choose to always smoke cigarettes or eat bad foods? You will suffer negative health consequences.

Because of their self-centered concentration, bad leaders have the power to influence others without regard for accountability or integrity.

Good leaders have visions that benefit everyone. By example, good leaders have understood the effectiveness of guiding rather than controlling others.

Understanding oneself is the first step in becoming a good leader. An excellent leader sets an example for others to follow. Who in their right mind will want to trust you to lead if your life demonstrates that you lack integrity, vision, and you are full of fear and doubt?

Leadership is 'caught' rather than 'taught.' What I mean is that we build our leadership skills through studying other leaders' actions and the impact of those actions on the people around us." In the Sage's vivid dream, he stops educating the group.

The sound of ships whistleblowing and cheering jolts WizdomTalk awake in the present day. He grinned as he remembered a place previously known as Sumer.

Unleash Your Vision

MICRONESIA

WizdomTalk awoke in the present day as the ship's stopovers were notified by a whistle. The Sage notices the white crystal sand and magnificent blue coral reefs that encircle Micronesia's gorgeous islands.

The Killer Whale makes daily stops for viewing on the islands of Palau, Chuuk, Yap, Kosrae, Pohnpei, Kiribati, Nauru, and the Marshall Islands. The natives greet you with a cheerful wave. They have tanned and copper-toned complexions, as well as straight and wavy hair.

The locals wear bright traditional clothing and dance to their music. Tourists are offered exotic fruits, coconuts, breadfruits, and seashells.

"Eat me, I am SO-SO Delicious!" the sweet aroma of ripe mangoes and pineapples seems to say in the breeze.

"Wow! What a lovely location!" WizdomTalk exclaims. As the Killer Whale docks in Guam to restock its supplies, People were giggling as tourists bravely parasail across the deep blue sea.

WizdomTalk disembarked to take in the island's sights. He met Lourdes, Guam's first female governor and is greeted with smiles by the locals. WizdomTalk discovered a plethora of ethnic groups, customs, and interesting things for travelers to enjoy.

WizdomTalk said his goodbyes and thanked the Guamanians for their hospitality when it was time to leave for Saipan.

Passengers could see large polka-dotted passenger balloons soaring through the dense white clouds as the ship reached Saipan in the Northern Mariana Islands.

The ship's passengers were awestruck as they saw swordfish leap from the Marianas Trench. Tourists later basked in the warmth of the sun in the cool of the afternoon.

The beautiful and serene backdrop immediately conjures up images of 'Paradise on Earth.' "Hafa Adai" and "Tirow," which mean "welcome" in their original Chamorro and Carolinian languages, are used to pleasantly greet all visitors in the Mariana Islands.

Dr. Ada and Dr. Rita noted educator explained to visitors. "In March 1521, Spanish explorer Ferdinand

Magellan discovered the Mariana Islands. The wreckage of the Manila Galleon Santa Margarita, which sank in 1600, is the only tangible evidence of Spain's landing on Saipan.

Survivors of the shipwreck remained among the Chamorros until they were rescued years later. Expeditions have been dispatched to the Mariana Islands by the governments of Spain, Germany, Japan, and the United States. The island's customs and languages were heavily influenced by these cultures.

People from the Caroline Islands in Micronesia arrived later in canoes, bringing with them their own language and culture. The Carolinian sailors were known for being skilled sea navigators.

Guam, Rota, Tinian, and Saipan are the four inhabited islands of the Mariana Islands. The Chamorro and Carolinian peoples are very smart and welcoming. They have religious values and strong family ties. Despite their sedate laid-back way of living, they certainly knew how to have a fiesta!

The Islanders get together for a Super Fiesta annually. Locals from Guam would gather on the beach at night to create a large campfire, play their ukuleles and guitars, and dance. Bluefin Tuna and Mahi-Mahi fish were brought in by anglers from Tinian's island to be barbecued over an open fire pit.

Mangoes, coconuts, papaya, bananas, vegetables, and jasmine rice were brought in by local farmers from Rota and Tinian for the Super Fiesta.

This year's magnificent event served as a cultural and educational opportunity. Major General Bain, a retired general, planned the event.

Beautiful and hardworking people from other Micronesia islands and other countries were also present. The diversity of each culture was accentuated by a plethora of dancers and singers, as well as a dizzying display of food.

The heady perfume of such delectable food, and the vibrant cultural garb threw even the sharks in the area into a frenzy. The island's tourist economy benefited from this celebration."

Unleash Your Vision

MAJOR GENERAL BAIN

Major General Bain, a retired military commander based in Saipan, is an Australian native. He had bought two modest hotels and eateries on Saipan and Guam's adjacent islands after his retirement. Because of his philosophy, the General's companies were successful, and he was known as an island Sage.

The local Chamorro and Carolinian people adored and respected the General, especially the children. The General had invited his mentor, WizdomTalk, to this year's Super Fiesta, so this fiesta was extra special.

The Mariana Islanders had spent time and effort arranging this event. The next day, the General intended to meet with the local leaders. However, a wicked enemy known as Dark Shadows has arrived on the islands, to the General's surprise. He was hiding in the shadows, waiting to show his true colors.

The Micronesia and Mariana Islands were so delightful that even Dark Shadows had to admit it! Dark Shadows was a tall, unpleasant older man with a red turban, a narrow nose, and green and yellow stains on his teeth.

His clothing was filthy and smelled sulfurous. Dark Shadows did not seem to fit in with the rest of the world's beauty. As a result, he hid beneath the massive green leaves of a large coconut tree. Dark Shadows was a clever man, but he had a habit of using his brilliance to sow discord and sorrow.

He had not bothered Major General Bain and WizdomTalk for years. Dark Shadows relished the occasion as he designed his strategy against his adversaries. He had learnt from experience to be very crafty and careful when preparing against them.

Dark Shadows was a very unpredictable and dangerous predator. Dark Shadows has unfortunately shown to be an ever-present, wicked, and persistent entity who only embraced those who served him!

UNLEASH YOUR VISION

The General and a group of community leaders were wandering around the Saipan Botanical Gardens one bright and sunny morning when they came across a Cockatoo Parrot chained to a bench. "Unleash me!" squawks the colored bird repeatedly. "Release me!"

The parrot's owner, Clyde, is a carnival worker who trained the bird to say these phrases. Even though the parrot is his source of income, he regularly mocked and teased it. Clyde was a depraved individual who thought his treatment of the bird was amusing. The General took a compassionate attitude towards the bird and began to pet it.

Surprisingly, the parrot began to speak to the community leaders, saying, "Medically, someone's vision must be 20/20 to be considered flawless.

You will always repeat the past if you do not have a 20/20 vision for your life or community. You will never achieve your full potential without 20/20 vision. True 20/20 vision is always based on one's reason for existing on this planet.

You were not thrown upon the world at random. In the eyes of the Creator, you are one-of-a-kind, a masterpiece. Always keep in mind that everyone and everything has a specific function.

You must first define your vision for it to mirror what you desire in life. As you can see, I am confined to the bench. I yearn for freedom, just as your inner visions yearn for it. Our ideas and dreams must be let loose to begin the process of realizing them.

I would like you to consider the following three questions: Do you have any idea what makes you happy in life? Is your life a reflection of your desires? What is your life's vision or fantasy?"

The Cockatoo gets deafeningly quiet. "To materialize your visions or dreams, they must align with your emotions and your actions," the Cockatoo adds. "Here's a way you can use to figure out what your true mission and vision are.

Please pay close attention to the story I am about to tell you. Assume you have inherited or won a hefty sum of money and are now instantaneously affluent. I am sure that primarily, you would want to pamper your family and friends by purchasing attractive items for them.

You may decide to purchase a larger home or travel around the world. You would even put a large chunk of your windfall into stocks and bonds and live off the interest!

You may decide to donate money to charities to assist those in need. However, once the excitement wears off, you will discover that, though not guaranteed, you can only live one day at a time.

Now that your circumstances have altered, what would you do with your time? What would you do if you had complete freedom to do whatever you wanted? What is it that you genuinely care about? Would you consider starting a new company? Would you consider creating a software to assist others? Would you return to school to master a new skill? Would you like to construct something?

Would you rather write a song or a book? Could you use the time to produce a new idea? Would you like to learn more to become more enlightened? Would you become more health-conscious and educate others how to do the same? Could you be an advocate for a group of people who are underserved?

There are plenty of options! You open the door to your inner purpose as you begin to answer these questions, and you may begin to unleash your vision." The bird went silent.

The President of the Federated States of Micronesia, the Governor of the Northern Mariana Islands, and the Governor of Guam all walked over to the Cockatoo and released it with immense compassion.

Their bold act was also significant, as if they were releasing the vision of their islanders as well. The gathering stood there in awe as the parrot flew high towards its dreams of freedom.

"Through WIZDOMPOWER!" stated Major General Bain, "you will learn how to unleash your thoughts and dreams and live to your full potential!"

The General later informed the island leaders that WizdomTalk would like to speak via satellite at the World Youth Summit 20/25.

He then approached them and requested authorization to broadcast live from Guam, Saipan, and Micronesia.

The President and Governors were ecstatic to participate and promote their cultures and islands around the world.

The General relaxed in the pleasant breeze beneath a coconut tree near the garden, after his speech. Three ripe coconuts suddenly fell from the tree and landed on the General's head.

Unleash Your Vision

As his mind wandered, he began to smile, while being slightly annoyed. He began to think about WizdomTalk, his mentor.

The Babylonian Cartel was formulating a nefarious plot halfway around the world in Abuja, Nigeria's Millennium Park, unbeknownst to The General.

BE A DREAMMAKER

The night sky was beautiful and full of white and blue shooting stars as the audience began to gather. The conversation began when a young boy named Eduardo inquired of Major General Bain, "Is there a difference between visions and dreams?"

"Wonderful question!" The General said. "It's obvious you've been paying attention!" The General proceeded, tugging Eduardo's ear, and rewarded him with candy.

The General continued and said, "Dreams in the form of mental images and thoughts can occur when you are asleep or awake, my friends.

Some people have regular dreams. Some people believe that they will never dream. A dream can also frequently serve as a window into our true desires.

When you create a plan to attain your objectives, your vision begins to take shape. Perceptions about finishing school, inventing something, starting a job, or helping your family or community may be formed.

Personal dreams are like floating kites that will fly away if not anchored with a plan and ambition.

Knowledge and innovation provide a solid foundation on which to build your plans. Your ability to achieve your objectives will be aided by your belief and confidence in your vision. You will follow others if you do not have a personal vision.

It all starts with you as a visionary for your own life. Even if your goals appear unattainable, a true vision is a dream with established tactics or plans on how to achieve your goals.

Visionaries have no qualms about letting their gut feelings lead them. They use the lessons they gain along the way to success, and learn from their experiences, including mistakes. You are all incredible visionaries! Never give up your dreams, and constantly employ your Creative Imagination!"

IMAGINATIVE CREATIVITY

Despite the dark and wet weather, the islanders remained cheerful and alert. Dark Shadows, unfortunately, did as well! As he stood in the village, Major General Bain clicked his heels and gave the throng a contemplative glance. Instantly, the islanders' minds were transferred to 1933 Europe, where they were seeing a political gathering in progress.

The people who resided there were well-educated and skilled in a variety of fields. As soon as the speaker approached the podium, the audience became silent. The crowd erupted in applause when the speaker raised his hand.

According to the General, "Take a look! The audience is made up of highly educated individuals, some of whom function as puppets in the hands of the dictator in front of them.

As he shouts and gestures, the speaker is a fascinating figure, telling the German people what they must do to realize his ideals of strength and prosperity.

Adolf Hitler is the name of this ruler. He did not tell the German people, though, how much it would cost them as a nation. He was asking German citizens to give up their will and creative imagination through his demands.

Hitler, who was both an artist and an author, is adept at using language and imagery to impose his perverse views. Hitler, however, did not begin his political career with malice in mind.

He wanted to be a good, uplifting force for his nation's people at the start of his administration. Unfortunately, as Hitler's desire for power developed, his creative imagination became distorted."

The people of the island are astounded at how easy this could happen and how one man could control so many people's minds.

The General went on to say: "Everyone has the ability to use their imagination creatively. You can employ creative imagination, unlike animals who lack creativity and are directed solely by instinct.

Everything that exists is the result of a person's imagination. We relinquish our destiny and future to others when we are unable to use our vision as a creative force in our life.

There are many people in the world who, like painters, utilize their imagination to create the world. In each situation, people must choose between doing good, to assist humanity, and doing evil, to oppress others.

Their impact on the world may seem typically modest, yet it may be enormous. For example, our frequent exposure to forms of social and other types of media such as television, radio, movies, music, books, literature, and the Internet shapes our attitudes about religion, politics, success, beauty, sexuality, and healthcare.

DO NOT WORRY if you are concerned about your reality being placed in the hands of others!!! You may create the future you want for yourself and others by using your creative imagination.

In a variety of settings, the power of positive, creative thinking has been demonstrated. Positive thought naturally aids healing in the human body, according to research. The Creator offers you the assurance you need to allow your imagination to run wild, as well as the power to create and live an abundant life."

"What is innovation?" Dr. Fred Hill inquired jokingly. "It indicates I want a vacation!" Francis Palacios Hill said as she hurled a rose at her husband and smacked him in the head. The islanders burst out laughing.

Then General Bain explained, "Innovation is a process utilized to transfer an idea or original thought into a reproducible value. This might lead to the development of a product or service that meets the needs of the consumer market. Remember that innovation is the result of a creative imagination and should be followed by a well-thought-out action plan.

Now go somewhere peaceful, close your eyes, and use your imagination to construct the world you wish to live in.

Can you tell me about your dream or ambition?" The islanders closed their eyes, drifted off to sleep, and awoke on their island, which had turned sunny and bright, much like their futures!

WHAT IS YOUR DREAM?

General Bain and WizdomTalk went for a stroll on the island of Saipan on this bright and sunny day. They came to a San Antonio elementary school and inquired about visiting. Mr. Demapan, the vice principal, was nice enough to invite them to visit.

Mr. Demapan started speaking to a school assembly. He inquired of his students, "What is your life's dream, primary objective, or ambition? Consider that for a moment?

Everyone has one, whether it is a good one or a bad one. It makes no difference how old you are. Do you want to work your way up the corporate ladder as a company executive?

Do you want to start or grow your own company? Do you wish to get a college diploma after graduating from high school? Would you want to start a nonprofit to help animals or the homeless, the environment or youngsters, the disabled or the elderly?

Do you aspire to work as a doctor, nurse, technician, or research scientist in the medical field? Would you want to work as a computer programmer, software developer, or graphic designer in the technology field?

Did you consider working as a teacher or counselor in a primary, secondary, or high school. Do you want to teach at a community college or a university? Would you like to demonstrate your abilities or crafts? Could you aspire to work in the government or the military?

Are you interested in becoming a minister, priest, imam, rabbi, missionary, or religious worker in the clergy? Do you wish to pursue a career as a professional athlete?

Are you creative and can produce innovative ideas or solve challenges? Are you an aspiring writer, singer, dancer, performer, or visual artist who wants to broaden your horizons?

Do you want to work in travel and aviation so you may tour the world and learn about diverse cultures? It is possible that the list might go on and on!

But, please, do not fantasize about your future. Act right now! Always keep in mind that setting goals is a necessary part of every desire or aspiration. "

MILLENNIUM PARK

The Babylonian Cartel meets today at Millennium Park in Abuja, Nigeria's capital. The gorgeous park, created by an Italian architect, attracts visitors from all over the world. The Millennium Park is brimming with unpolluted nature, including native plants, a rainforest, a butterfly greenhouse, and a tropical bird sanctuary.

A large river runs through Millennium Park, dividing it into two sections. The cartel members travel along a paved path with Roman white stones as they enter Millennium Park in their luxurious limousines.

Members of the cartel could see the pavilion where they planned to meet. When they arrived, Dark Shadows was already there. The group, fortunately, did not need to plug their noses because his stink was confined by a lovely breeze. WizdomTalk was moving around in the group, invisible, and listening to their conversation.

The Babylonian Cartel soon got down to business. Countess Colleen had a lovely appearance. She is one of the Cartel's most intelligent members. She took a step forward and started to speak, " During the night, I had a thought. We should invite Ingrid, the previous Prime Minister, to join El Marco on stage and support him. She can provide a feminine element, wisdom, and be an authority figure at the youth summit.

She holds a doctorate in education from one of the world's most elite universities. She is also a university professor and a previous head of state from a powerful country. Furthermore, she was awarded the Nobel Prize many years ago, and you cannot compete with that kind of recognition.

Prime Minister Ingrid will accept our offer of assistance because she understands that she owes our cartel for assisting in her election and keeping her scandals hidden from public view. We can arrange for El Marco and Prime Minister Ingrid to speak right before WizdomTalk since we have influence in the media and at the World Youth Summit 20/25.

We already know what WizdomTalk talks about, and he is always dressed in an unflattering manner. He has the appearance of a fool and a clown, and he smells like peppermint. As a result, he and his antics will soon be dismissed by the youth and their parents. We can finally put a stop to him.

Because our speakers will speak before the Sage, we will be able to launch an early attack against his WIZDOMPOWER'S philosophy, notions, tricks, and bizarre anecdotes.

El Marco and the former Prime Minister will misrepresent WizdomTalk's character, twisting this rogue's rationale into fables. They will make him look like the imbecile, knucklehead, and fool he is.

All satellite and internet communications emanating from the island will be turned off anyway."

Dark Shadows is happy, nods, and flashes a wicked grin after hearing this, and the group glows with great approval. Dark Shadows said, "Let's do it."

Dr. Cadaver was a cartel member and corrupt scientist. "MetaMutate-25 will be ready to be inserted into the Summit attendees' gift bags next week," he stated as he stood up. Then clapping came from a Cartel member.

Dark Shadows, on the other hand, remembered his humiliation at the hands of WizdomTalk in a location once known as Sumer, and he became enraged.

PART II

VALLEY OF THE KINGS

The desert air in Egypt is hot and sticky, and insects are buzzing everywhere. When traveling Egypt's Nile River, you will come across ancient Egyptian cultural sites. The Egyptian Pharaohs were buried in the Valley of the Kings and the Pyramids of Giza.

The World Youth Summit 20/25 will be held today in the Valley of the Kings, in a huge, air-conditioned glass edifice. "Knowledge is Power" is the summit's theme. Thousands of talented young people from all around the world began to pour into the venue for the World Youth Summit 20/25.

Each young person was given a gift bag when they arrived. These bags are filled with high-priced things and products. The youth are unaware that their gift bags have been contaminated with MetaMutate-25. A terrible global pandemic will be caused by this time-released virus.

They were a colorful group of young people that represented various nations. They arrived full of zeal and anticipation. This collection of young leaders has one thing in common: they all want to make the world a better place.

The youth are ecstatic to see and hear Prime Minister Ingrid and El Marco in person. Young people believed they could learn from these so-called world icons since they were well-known and approachable.

Prime Minister Ingrid and El Marco sit chit-chatting in the speaker's waiting area. A couple of cartel members enter the room and shut the door behind them so no one could bother them.

WizdomTalk had not yet arrived at the Saipan festival, they reasoned. Earlier, the Sage had sneaked into the speaker's room, hidden a camera and microphone, and connected it to the event monitor.

The gathering turned raucous when Egypt's President welcomed the guests and cracked a few jokes. "El Marco, Prime Minister Ingrid, please come out," they continue to yell.

CONTROLLED OPPOSITION

The yells were heard by the speakers, El Marco, and Prime Minister Ingrid, who enjoyed the attention and ornamentation.

Elliot is a member of the Babylonian Cartel. He has extraordinary abilities and uses them to hypnotize El Marco and Prime Minister Ingrid while showing them a laboratory. He then transported their minds to the laboratory full of mice.

The scientists were putting control opposition to the test there. A large banner hangs over two large doors, which the two observed, "SECRETS" and "WORLD CONTROL".

A big glass cage with a staircase was visible to El Marco and Prime Minister Ingrid. Food was placed at the

Unleash Your Vision

top of the stairwell. There were also twenty-one hungry white mice in the glass box.

The white mice were adorable, according to Prime Minister Ingrid. The experiment was about to begin, and the room fell silent.

The hungry mice have undoubtedly noticed the food and were overjoyed. The scientists allowed only one mouse at a time to climb the steps. The mice were drenched with water when they got to the top of the stairwell and the meal. This cycle continued and the mice became frustrated.

During the next experiment, the scientists put twenty-one hungry black mice into the glass box to join the twenty-one white mice. After that, the scientists made each black mouse climb up the stairwell.

The white mice became angry and assaulted all twenty-one black mice, preventing them from climbing the stairs. One black mouse was starving and determined to get his reward, so he fought back and made it to the top, where he ate a nice meal.

At that point, Elliot's phone started ringing with multiple calls, but he does not want to be disturbed, so he shuts it off. Elliot makes the following announcement: "We, the Babylonian Cartel, are like these scientists, and you are all part of us.

Yes, Prime Minister, I realize you already know what I am about to tell El Marco, but please bear with me. Conditioning is a negative sort of control, and the experiment you just witnessed is an example of it.

This type of conditioning is still used in the world today. Advertisements, music, entertainment, education, jails, the military, government, political movements, and religious cults all use conditioning.

Dark Shadows, the Babylonian Cartel, and others who believe and act like us are represented by the scientists. The food in the glass box symbolizes an achievement or a prize.

Controlled resistance, negative suggestions, manipulation, and hurdles to a person's rewards or aspirations are represented by the water dousing.

The forty-one mice depict society's indoctrinated and scared citizens. The youth with whom you will speak, we want them to continue to be influenced. The final mouse depicts a vibrant individual with ambitions and a passion who overcomes obstacles to become a DreamMaker.

We do not want the youth you are about to speak with to become DREAMMAKERS because that would jeopardize our hidden purpose.

Please note that, except for one mouse, all the mice's brains perished first, followed by physical death from hunger on the same day. This is because they accepted our fantasies about their lives as well as the challenges posed by these scientists.

The DREAMMAKER mouse, on the other hand, lived and learnt to think clearly and worked hard to achieve his goals. Now, El Marco, please go out there and engage these youth.

You will get them ready for Prime Minister Ingrid. Let us now perform the final rituals for these dumb mice. We have assembled here today for these unlucky mice; dearly beloved...."

El Marco, Prime Minister Ingrid, and the members of the Cartel all chuckled. When the party awoke, they observed that there were no more shouts.

Then one of the cartel members walked into the room and unplugged the camera and microphone, saying, "Elliot, we tried calling you. Why didn't you pick up the phone?

The event monitor mysteriously transmitted what you showed El Marco and Prime Minister Ingrid to the summit regarding the scientists and mice, but not on the Internet or television."

El Marco felt humiliated and refused to speak to the young people. The Prime Minister, on the other hand, is not fazed because she knows how to manipulate words and circumstances. She had been a successful leader for a long time, and these young people were like her children.

She told the members of the Babylonian Cartel, "I'm going to let these youth' imaginations go wild with possibilities for the future. They'll forget what they saw on the event monitor today."

"Who could have done this to us?" El Marco wondered. "WizdomTalk," they all chorused.

Elliot inquired of the Prime Minister about her plans for sharing with the youth. "GLOBAL HAPPINESS and TRANSHUMANISM," she said.

"What is that?" El Marco inquired.

She said, "El Marco, do not be scared. Please come up to the stage with me and find out."

INGRID AND EL MARCO

It is showtime, and there was a knock at the door. The speakers are escorted onto the platform by security. There was no pleasant welcome, but there were a lot of boos. The youth are enraged by what they have witnessed on the event monitor.

It took a while for the crowds to quiet down. The Prime Minister began speaking after she was introduced and given honors. "My dear young folks, what you saw on the monitors was unattractive, but it was not genuine. We were merely trying to figure out what you were thinking. We would never harm you intentionally."

At that point, Latin music started playing, and the Prime Minister began to twerk and dance with the crowd.

The crowd erupted as El Marco unexpectedly appeared on stage and began singing and dancing with her. Elliot joined Prime Minister Ingrid and El Marco on stage after thirty minutes of nonstop music.

Prime Minister Ingrid finally started speaking to the television and internet audiences. "Look at my friend Elliott, who is holding a large model spaceship," she murmured quietly in a calming tone. "Now concentrate your attention on the image of the green spacecraft. Let us take a mental journey together in a space rocket to learn about TRANSHUMANISM and GLOBAL HAPPINESS."

"What is Transhumanism and Global Happiness, and where are we going, Madam?" questions Cheryl from the audience.

"Global Happiness" is defined by the Prime Minister as "all classes of people living in peace and harmony with one another. They work together to share and govern their mutual interests and fates."

She went on to say, "the future globe is expected to be borderless, which would allow governments to transport commodities, services, and capital with fewer restrictions.

A global culture, social lifestyle, and political ideology will unite the entire world. Individual ideas and a sovereign nation, including its institutions, will be superseded by this.

People will be considered solely as commodities, rather than as human beings, with a focus on their ability to generate skills or labor in the global economy. People will make decisions on a level playing field on planet Earth, with no commitment to their neighbors or their own country's citizens.

Using Transhumanism and Global Happiness, we will travel into the future to the year 2035 to see if humanity is progressing or regressing."

YEAR – 2035

The members of the audience were off in their imaginations in the future, down a brilliant tunnel of lights, as Elliot pointed out and mass hypnotized the audience. When they arrived in the year 2035, they began to travel across the world in a miraculous manner.

National boundaries, sovereignty, and separate cultures were no longer apparent to the spectators. Even in industrialized countries, highly skilled people appeared to work for little pay. Many minor countries have been invaded by foreigners seeking greater economic opportunities. Multinational corporations own the most major business enterprises. Technology was continuously monitoring everyone.

Unleash Your Vision

The audience was taken away as they observed cars silently speeding through the sky, no longer tied to the ground. Sleek trains traveled at great speeds over and underwater, with no tracks, from one country to the next.

Some of the humans of 2035 appeared to have been cloned and were devoid of individuality. Strange-looking wild animal crossbreeds arose out of nowhere, yet they were domesticated and had microchips embedded in them.

The fact that people can communicate with these animals and were not afraid astounded the audience. Because everything was kept digitally, there were no more books, periodicals, or newspapers.

Farmers were shown complaining to business representatives in front of an audience. Farmers were compelled to purchase genetically modified organisms (GMO) seeds and fertilizers to raise their harvests. The growers' dilemma is that these genetic seeds did not develop seeds of their own. Many vegetables, fruits, and meats are genetically engineered these days.

Scientists are still debating whether these foods are healthy now. Even though governments must authorize them for consumption, future farmers believe that to do business and exist, they are at the mercy of agribusiness and pharmaceutical firms.

Giant conglomerate corporations control all commercial operations, allowing tiny entrepreneurs to own and operate little businesses in the marketplace. People's daily movements, purchasing habits, lifestyle choices, and daily lives are observed and tracked on a supercomputer database.

When the group visited the grocery stores, there were only robots serving the customers, no human employees. The shoppers did not use money and credit cards. Machines simply scanned microchips in their hands or on their foreheads. Because human bodies were microchipped and used for communication and networking, there was no more need for cell phones or laptop computers.

When the party visited factories, malls, and other workplaces, they discovered the saddest thing: they were all ran by robots and were devoid of people. Everything and everyone were connected, synchronized, and wireless.

The Prime Minister declared. "What you have just seen is Transhumanism in action. Transhumanism is a philosophical, scientific, and intellectual movement that argues for altering the human experience now and in the future using creative, sophisticated technology and research.

Transhumanism's true purpose is to improve human intelligence and physiology. Transhumanists aspire to achieve a phenomenon known as synchronicity. Synchronicity is a system in which its components are intertwined and act in concert with one another. It may indicate a better approach to regulate and control society for those who embrace Transhumanism.

Artificial intelligence (AI), deoxyribonucleic acid (DNA) modification, microchips, and robotics will all be used in transhumanism to revolutionize civilization. Wild and domestic animals, plants, fruits, and vegetables will be crossbred. Transhumanism aspires to synchrony and success.

AI is a method for transferring and storing all of humanity's intelligence into supercomputer databases. AI connects this stored intelligence to the human experience. When you call customer service, for example, AI is at work. To address your needs, a computer asks you a series of questions that are subject to the human experience. This is a simple example of artificial intelligence.

The goal of transhumanism is to create a utopia for people on Earth. Imagine living to be 150 years old or, on a conscious level, thinking as quickly as a computer. People in the future may have eagle-like vision or superhuman strength. Scientists could mass-produce human organ replacements using stem cells and DNA manipulation. To some, all of this is undoubtedly fantastic.

However, there is opposition to transhumanism. Dissidents argue that man is attempting to be the Creator. Others argue that because Transhumanism crosses humans, plants, and animals, it is an insult to religion and environment.

Many diseases will be eradicated, according to the Transhumanists, and everyone's life will be longer, healthier, and better. But at what cost to humanity's experience. Will many people become worthless eaters and finally extinct since robots will be doing much of the work?"

Suddenly, there is a tremendous deal of ambiguity and a palpable sense of foreboding about the future. "My friends, isn't this is the future you would want for yourself and your loved ones?" the Prime Minister asked, beaming enthusiastically. Because the youth were perplexed, no one said anything.

Despite their youth, the audience recognized that people's livelihoods and existence could be replaced in the future.

Prime Minister Ingrid expressed her gratitude to the international public for their attention. Then she remarked. "I normally don't query the summit organizers about how they choose their speakers. However, WizdomTalk, the keynote speaker, appears to be an unqualified clown. His thinking and knowledge are out of date.

All you have to do is look at his clothing." Do not be deceived by his theatrics. This man, I must add, is a moron and he is demented. He has no official education, and no one is aware of his full history. As far as I could tell, he is not trustworthy.

This old man is only useful while he is asleep! His lips move a lot when he delivers falsehood, so you can usually tell when he is lying. If you are a parent watching, please turn off your media during this part of the summit. Your youngsters will be misled by this character's thinking." She grinned, crossed her arms, and waited for five minutes, silently, for the audience to react.

Dark Shadows and the Babylonian Cartel were ecstatic by her performance. Then the Prime Minister Ingrid exclaims, "Let me pass you over to the Mayor of the Island of Saipan via satellite. The keynote speaker, WizdomTalk, was too afraid to attend the World Youth Summit 20/25 in person. The mayor can now present the rogue."

However, after hearing this, 98 percent of the summit's parents and youngsters wanted to switch off their televisions and computers and stop attending. Furthermore, the Babylonia Cartel had cut off satellite and internet connectivity from Saipan.

But, unbeknownst to the Cartel, WizdomTalk had miraculously restored global satellite and internet communications. As a result, the entire globe was watching. However, the massive live audiences in Egypt and Saipan had gotten hungry and thirsty for lunch and began to boo WizdomTalk. The crowd went completely silent as they smelled the peppermint, yet there was no one on the monitor.

Unleash Your Vision

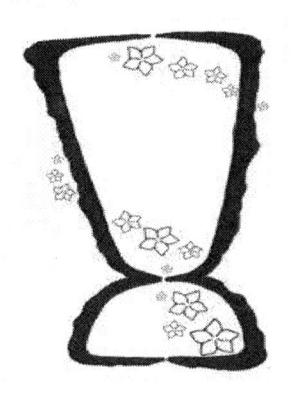

SAIPAN

Friday was a fantastic day for a get-together! The sky was a brilliant blue, and the sun was shining brightly. The indifferent crowd at the World Youth Summit 20/25 grew impatient as they waited for their keynote speaker to come on the screens via satellite from Saipan.

They inquired, "Where is this, man?" As Saipan's Mayor Apatang approached the stage, the crowd fell silent. When the much-loved Mayor took the microphone, the island throng erupted in applause.

The mayor greeted the crowd with 'Hafa Adai' and 'Tirow' which meant 'welcome' in his native languages. Mayor Apatang said, "Ladies and Gentlemen, I would like to present you to the mystical, enchanting, and enlightening WizdomTalk. He came to us from the Middle East, a place which was originally known as Babylon and Sumer.

He will show you how to unleash your vision and get power over the next few days. He claims that through what he refers to as WIZDOMPOWER, he can assist us in realizing our ultimate purpose in life." As they waited for the guest speaker, WizdomTalk, to come, the laughing crowd buzzed with expectation.

"Where is this fellow?" the mayor asks, whispering in Major General Bain's ear. A screeching sound is immediately heard by the live crowds on the islands and in Egypt.

The delicious cologne of peppermint was carried to Saipan and Egypt by a southern trade wind. Soft Middle Eastern drums started playing out of nowhere. "An ancient camel is usually smarter than a young goat!" says a mystery baritone voice over both crowds.

Because no one was visible, both groups were bewildered and terrified. Then, suddenly, white smoke filled both stages, and a young man playing African drums emerged on both stages at the same time.

He was dressed in a black tuxedo with a ruffled white shirt and a Middle Eastern scarf with red speckles. The onlookers began to snigger when they spotted his backward baseball cap and big purple tennis sneakers.

The drums then started beating on their own, producing an upbeat island music. WizdomTalk began by combining an African and island rhythm with the Spanish Cha–Cha.

When a Mercedarian nun, Sister Maria, joined WizdomTalk on stage to dance, the audience erupted in laughter at the spontaneous performance. The stunned Mayor passed out when the General began to dance!

The joyous audience exploded with laughter once more because of this drama! When the Governor tried to intercede, the strong peppermint cologne overcame him, and he had to be carried off the stage.

The Egyptian President, his officers, and the summit officials could not stop themselves from dancing too. Prime Minister Ingrid blacked out, startled by the activity! Egypt's young crowd erupted with even more laughter. When El Marco tried to intervene, the drumbeat overtook him, and he began to dance.

"An old camel is always smarter than a young goat," said WizdomTalk the General's mentor, said again in a muffled voice. The global audience began to ponder the parable's implications. WizdomTalk froze in place after minutes of silence.

[CHALLENGE ACCEPTED]

The keynote speaker began to sweat, he unfroze after 15 minutes. The stunned audience could not say anything. "The proverb, 'An old camel is always smarter than a young goat' suggests that, in most cases, an older person is wiser than a younger one, due to their experiences and the life lessons they have acquired," WizdomTalk told the world's youngsters.

"How old are you, Sir?" someone shouted from the audience. "I am ancient, but I am still a stylish and trendy person," WizdomTalk said with a smile and a flash of his teeth. The audience laughed. "My beloved young people and others who are listening," WizdomTalk continued, "I am a Sage, which means I am an outstanding teacher and mentor. My strength comes from The Most High, and I am wise.

Prime Minister Ingrid and her allies offered you what could be considered a well-thought-out plan. I am not even going to respond to all she said. I will defer to your wise judgment in deciding how you wish to live now and in the future.

Unleash Your Vision

WISDOM is what I teach, and it is what directs, protects, and innovates. Prime Minister Ingrid and the Babylonian Cartel lie, dominate, and manipulate people to further their own selfish goals. Unlike them, I do not have a hidden agenda. I simply want the best for you.

People that listen to me will become members of the DREAMMAKERS CLUB, an incredible and wonderful society. This club's members will make a positive difference in their lives and the world around them. Prepare to discover life lessons through fables, travel, mysteries, and values while encountering fascinating personalities along the route."

The Sage then lowered his head and takes a little nap. WizdomTalk woke up and continued speaking after Major General Bain delicately sprinkled water on his mentor's face. "Please, instead of disdain, have a heart or genuine aspirations for humanity. People are taught that the Earth is home to a diverse range of ethnic races, however this is not the case.

This, instead, was merely a man's idea. Humanity, which comes in a variety of colors, is the sole true race of people. No color is greater to another in humanity. History shows us that every so-called race has made a positive or negative contribution to humanity.

When Prime Minister Ingrid remarked, "Global Happiness is when all classes of people are in peace and harmony with one another, and they share and govern their common interests and destinies together." The Sage took a deep breath and continued, "Prime Minister Ingrid presented her erroneous viewpoint, and now I will present mine. You will be the one to decide who is telling the truth."

For a small group of people, GLOBAL HAPPINESS is an amazing notion. They want to have influence over billions of people, governments, trade, natural resources, and the media, or they want to be able to produce a global workforce at cheaper pay. It will limit or remove the authority of the independent nation state. It will also fail to preserve diverse cultures, languages, and traditional living systems such as education, religion, and local business.

Yes, I believe that some transhumanist technology, when applied properly to benefit humanity, is a lovely thing. Do you ever wonder why, despite all the new and exciting technologies, there are still no solutions for the deadly diseases?

Despite billions of dollars spent on research around the world, no treatment appears to have been discovered. Pharmaceutical corporations, on the other hand, can create and sell drugs that only allow patients to live with their illnesses.

Natural herbalists should be praised because they have used organic methods to cure terrible ailments, but they are hardly mentioned. Did you know that autos were powered by gasoline one hundred years ago, and still are today?

Unleash Your Vision

Someone must have invented an alternative fuel source, but you never hear about it. Is it possible that those in charge of specific areas of society want it that way? Why?

Keep in mind that you do not have to act like the mice in the experiment. You are human beings with abilities such as vision, power, and potential.

You should avoid being ruled by a system that is anti-human in nature. Did the Creator intend for everyone to have the same country, culture, religion, education, or monetary policy? Why would the Creator allow multiple languages, cultures, and nation-states?

The Creator's natural way of living is diametrically opposed to anything termed GLOBAL HAPPINESS.

These are the principles and talents you should employ to shape your life and the lives of others as future leaders and global citizens. Respect, Integrity, Accountability, Compassion, Spirituality, Excellence, Innovation, Productivity, and Stewardship are all crucial.

The unforgettable L-Factors at the end of my classes will summarize my answer to Prime Minister Ingrid's attack on me.

Through something called WIZDOMPOWER, I will begin to educate you on how to maintain your life's dreams and ambitions. I'm going to show you something amazing, and you're going to become a DREAMMAKER."

WizdomTalk wiggles his brows and clicks his fingers as he points upwards to the ceiling. Suddenly, the air was filled with white doves. They were holding lunch with cold drinks in brown baskets.

The doves began to deliver the food baskets to the crowd in a magical manner. What was incredible and mysterious is that white doves with brown lunch baskets emerged in all the homes of those who were being followed by various media throughout the world.

Suddenly, there was a huge void. The Sage yawned and fell asleep on his stage drums. Then, on the display, a message emerged that said, "See you after lunch, WINNERS."

"WOW! Who is this person?" exclaimed the audience. They had a good laugh and ate wonderful food.

Unleash Your Vision

YOU ARE BEAUTIFUL ISLANDS

A gusty breeze pushed the waves towards the San Antonio Beach the next afternoon. WizdomTalk was being followed by the people and visitors of Saipan. Many people started collecting seashells. One huge, colorful white seashell was discovered. Black Pearl inhabited it. Black Pearl, who sparkled and radiated elegance, began to speak without notice. "Do you ever see your island of beauty glow?" she asked the islanders and their visitors.

"Each of you is like an Island of Beauty!" she said. "An Island of Beauty represent your originality. Each of you, like the countless islands of the Earth, has your own distinct personality and beauty.

However, much as islands are linked under the sea by a single big solid rock, you are all linked by a common humanity."

"Your skin's varied hues resemble the vibrant life seen on islands all over the world. Like you, all islands have positive and negative characteristics.

Volcanoes erupt with such fury that they create islands. The forces that will help form your future are the vision and genius that you possess.

An island's life and beauty change throughout time. You, too, will need time to cultivate your abilities, intellect, and beauty. The beauty of an island is a gift from the gods, and every time you look in the mirror, you will witness an Island of Beauty glow."

"Let's learn more about Choice."

Black Pearl then winked at them, closed her eyes, and returned to her seashell. The satellites are following the Sage's every move.

BANZAI CLIFF: A CHOICE

A sense of serenity comes came over the mass of islanders when the powerful south wind stopped blowing and the air relaxed. The gathering is led by the General and WizdomTalk on a walk to Saipan's Banzai Cliff. The group was trailed by television cameras everywhere they went, so the entire world was watching.

Dark Shadows had hidden himself in the crowd to accompany them on this journey, being his usual cunning self.

He was ecstatic, and he looked forward to returning to Banzai Cliff because it represented one of his most heinous accomplishments to date!

While visitors continued to visit the cliff, locals were hesitant to do so because of the cliff's tragic legacy, known as *Suicide Cliff*. The General said via a giant bullhorn as he walks alongside the large crowd. "Not wanting to be left behind, many individuals follow the crowd. The crowd's 'actions' can be represented by current or popular thought and behavior in areas such as family, education, politics, relationships, and religion. Unwisely, many individuals accept this way of looking at the world without challenging or exploring its origins, meanings, or implications."

WizdomTalk yawned, and the sounds of drumming and sensuous Japanese music were heard unexpectedly. He began to dance with an imaginary partner in a mystical manner, then froze and fell asleep.

The islanders laughed as they wondered why he always fell asleep in the middle of a lesson.

WizdomTalk woke up minutes later, batting his eyes, and added, "Let us look at a World War II historical occurrence as an example. In 1944, American Navy ships assaulted Saipan's northern coast, where Japanese forces were stationed in strongholds. Local Japanese civilians were stationed on the enormous cliffs with the military.

The Japanese civilians had been residing in the Mariana Islands since 1918, when the islands were passed over to the Japanese government by the League of Nations during World War I.

The League of Nations was the precursor of the United Nations as we know it today.

The Japanese army inflicted destruction across the Pacific Rim and Asia after the attack on Pearl Harbor in Hawaii in 1941. The war's tide was turning, and the Japanese force was losing ground. The Japanese High Command on Saipan issued a declaration as a final act of resistance. Soldiers and people were ordered to commit 'Hari Kari,' or suicide, under this edict.

If seized, the American troops would mistreat the women, execute them, and devour the flesh of the surviving, according to the High Command. Many soldiers and people, believing this to be true, plunged from the cliffs onto massive rocks to meet their brute force's doom. Many Japanese did not die immediately, but instead languished in excruciating pain and agony for hours, if not days. Many of the victims thought this suicidal deed was extremely patriotic.

Banzai Cliff is the name for this location. This horrific occurrence was captured on video by American ships in the sea below and recorded for posterity.

During this time, the Japanese government's worldview resulted in the destruction of many places.

However, neither the Japanese Emperor nor any his top officers, society's upper crust, or war profiteers committed suicide. Why? Because leaders never follow in the footsteps of the masses!

Ordinary people suffer the most when they support those in authority, even when they are deceived. The tragedy at Banzai Cliff could have been prevented if the Japanese people had been aware of their own goals and plans.

Your lives are distinct from one another. You have control over your mind and purpose, which may or may not reflect the opinions of others around you. You have been given special abilities, extraordinary gifts, and a special destiny.

Your devotion and decisions should reflect your values, principles, and goals. We should always challenge orders that could jeopardize our safety or that of our family. Other thoughts or activities in the areas of relationships, spirituality, finance, business, community, and education can be included.

Remember that everyone, even those with the best of intentions, make errors. We reason based on our own views and experiences, but we are nonetheless capable of being 'dead' incorrect.

This is exactly what occurred at Banzai Cliff. Suicide is a final failure from which there is no recovery. It is frequently viewed as a selfish act because it may cause anguish to the relatives and friends of the departed. A person would certainly not wish to self-destruct before completing their goal.

The current Japanese government has caring, and innovative people who make a positive difference in the world. After the war, America assisted in the reconstruction of Japan, and it now has one of the world's largest economies.

You are an innovator as a DREAMMAKER, and you do not have to mindlessly follow the crowd, especially when it takes you to a cliff!"

"We will discuss 'Goal Setting' tomorrow."

Dark Shadows surely did not like what he heard. He covered his ears as he screamed. However, he was disappointed to find that no one had heard him.

TOOLS FOR GOAL SETTING

The group of islanders and guests strolled along the beach the next day to meet WizdomTalk at the Duty-Free Shoppers (DFS) store. Dr. Joyner, an elderly bodybuilder and health enthusiast, was exercising as they passed. They were perplexed as to how he stayed in shape and maintained the physique of a much younger man.

"I have a goal and a plan to stay in shape," Dr. Joyner stated after hearing their conversation. This is what you'll need to get anything done." The islanders and visitors bid their goodbyes after thanking him for his warmth and wisdom. Even though they had no idea about what he was talking.

They were surrounded by vibrant and gorgeous displays of high-end products as they entered the Duty-Free Shoppers store. Salespeople were busy attracting consumers as they plied their trade. As the group reached a DFS conference room, Marian, an executive, was energizing her team. "What will be the outcome for your life if you don't have a goal in sight?" she asked her colleagues.

WizdomTalk came just in time to hear the conversation with Marian and her staff. "It's fantastic to work hard, but it doesn't guarantee that you'll be successful," Marian argued passionately. "However, to be successful, you must not only work hard, but also efficiently and smartly."

"Others may exploit you by leveraging your talent and labor to their benefit if you do not perform these things. As you can see, a variety of things influence success. Setting goals is one of the most crucial. A goal is an aim that you wish to achieve, and a plan is a strategy for achieving that goal.

Setting goals is critical because it is difficult to achieve anything without them." Marian clarified. "Remember that you are accountable for the decisions you make and, as a result, for the rewards or repercussions of those actions, no matter how excellent or flawed they may be.

I would like to provide you a step-by-step guide to some of the most important aspects of goal setting and planning. This plan will not ensure success, but it will significantly lower the chances of failure.

This is a useful rule to remember as you begin to learn about goal setting and planning. Are the aims and plans I am setting advantageous to all parties involved?'

Only once you have answered yes to this question will you move on to the next level. These are steps for goal setting.

1. FEEL. Believe in yourself and your ability to do everything you set your mind to.

2. BELIEVE. Have faith in your ability to achieve whatever you set your mind to.

3. DESIRE. Make sure you have a compelling rationale for reaching your objective.

4. WRITE. Take some time to jot down all the benefits of reaching your goal. Your goal will become substantial and genuine once you have done this.

5. ESTABLISH A DEADLINE. Setting a deadline will motivate you to keep moving forward with your goal. Setting a deadline for the completion of your project will help you identify and prioritize tasks that must be completed before that deadline.

6. TROUBLE-SHOOT. Make a list of any hurdles you will have to overcome and write them down.

7. EVALUATE. Identify the resources (people, knowledge, and materials) that you will require to achieve your objective.

8. MAKE A STRATEGY. List, detail, and prioritize steps 1-7 above to develop a strategy for achieving your goal. Check to see if each phase is feasible!

9. MAKE USE OF YOUR IMAGINATION. Visualize how you want your objective to look once you have achieved it. It is important to have a vivid and clear mental image.

10. TENACIOUSNESS IS KEY. Maintain your fortitude by adhering to your plan and NEVER GIVING UP, even when hurdles or setbacks arise."

PLANNING

WizdomTalk joined the islanders at the airport the next day. He exclaimed, "All Aboard," as he stood next to a gigantic supersonic plane. The Sage's brows fluttered as he pointed to the East. The group arrived in the magnificent metropolis of Dubai in the United Arab Emirates in minutes.

The city was in a hot desert, surrounded by tall, ultra-modern skyscrapers. Carpenters and welders were among the construction personnel on the job. The islanders were on their way to view the sites.

As they approached a museum, they discovered a construction worker named Khalid working on a large building without safety equipment.

This was deemed silly and harmful by the children.

Crown Prince Mohammad stood nearby with a gathering of business leaders. He was the mastermind behind Dubai's new and better design.

He approached WizdomTalk and his posse. "Khalid did not take appropriate steps and plan for his safety," he argued, "so he would be unable to achieve his work goals.

If you do not have a strategy, you are setting yourself up to fail! You might have brilliant ideas and skills for realizing your ambitions. Even so, you will not be successful unless you have a clear and responsible plan.

The oil-rich United Arab Emirates was primarily desert and had no modern services until a few years ago. Even though we had a vision and the tools to establish a better society, it took years for it to happen.

Finally, once we had made up our minds and committed to our mission, we proceeded to devise a strategy. We have started to achieve our goals and more by putting our plan into action and strategically utilizing our resources! Dubai is now visited by people from all over the world." With a wink, he asked, "Isn't this amazing?"

"The following elements are crucial to good planning," the Crown Prince continued.

"1) To attain it, you must have a reasonable dream or objective.

2) To conduct your plan, you must have the requisite abilities, competence, and resources.

3) Your project must be trustworthy. This entails dealing with people in a fair and honest manner.

4) You must be accountable to yourself. This implies that you have a method for determining success or failure.

5) Your strategy must be flawless. This means you will aim for excellence rather than mediocrity.

6) You must be charitable. This entails treating everyone affected by your work with respect and compassion, including the environment.

Dubai is a dream, and I was a part of it," the Crown Prince continued. "Look around. Have you ever seen a city so contemporary and attractive anyplace else in the world?"

The group took another glance around, this time with a newfound sense of awe. They took in the tall structures, a fabricated island with luxurious hotels, and the searing desert in the background.

"What an impressive dream and plan!" said WizdomTalk. "Let us all go to the luxurious hotel on the fabricated island and spend the night!" The Islanders were overjoyed!

Unleash Your Vision

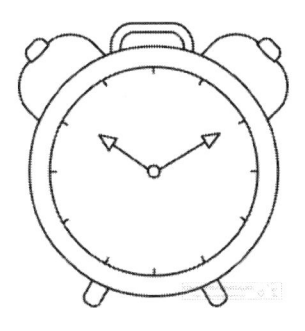

TIME MANAGEMENT

The sun was sinking today over the Marianas Trench, the world's deepest region of the ocean, at 35,000 feet. "Do you want to tour Big Ben?" asked a nicely dressed WizdomTalk to the stunned crowd of islanders.

"Who is Big Ben?" Soledad inquired.

"Let's see," WizdomTalk said as he clicks his heels to summon a magic carpet.

He exclaimed, "All aboard!" The islanders somehow landed in London, in front of a massive clock. He said, "Let me present you to Big Ben!" The group looked perplexed and nervously laughed.

"As you can see, I am a clock, and I represent TIME," Big Ben said as he walked and talked. "TIME is one of the most valuable commodities we possess. Everyone has been granted twenty-four hours a day to live, whether they are rich or poor, healthy, or not.

How you use and manage your time has an impact on your quality of life. People who have poor time management abilities experience a lot of stress in their lives. Setting goals, scheduling, and creating a realistic action plan are all necessary components of effective time management.

Time management can help you stay on track to achieving your objectives and desires in life. Consider sleeping for 16 hours every day. Would you be able to get a lot done? You would be well-groomed but less productive if you spent five hours a day grooming yourself in front of the mirror.

Consider how many hours you spend watching television or on social media as a kind of enjoyment. Do you believe this is particularly useful? If you want to live a balanced and productive life, time management is essential."

Then Big Ben started gonging loudly. WizdomTalk answered, "TIME!" when asked what the sound symbolized.

Unleash Your Vision

A BALANCED SUMO WINS!

The sea was calm and peaceful as the large white yacht, piloted by WizdomTalk, transported the islanders far north.

"Do you want to go to Tokyo?" The Sage asked the islanders. "Sure!" they exclaimed with glee.

"Hold on tight!" exclaimed WizdomTalk.

The journey was a little bumpy, but they made it to Japan in no time. The group went to attend a Sumo wrestling match at a local arena after a brief visit to an aquarium.

A soft-spoken Japanese woman started the conversation. "There is an interesting sport called Sumo wrestling here in Japan," she explained. "Sumo wrestlers are exceptional athletes who must eat a lot of food to stay in shape.

It is great drama as a Sumo enters the ring. They have little hair on their heads and wear colorful long robes. As they bow respectfully to their opponents, they appear healthy and confident. Despite their appearance of being overweight and out of shape, the wrestlers practice hard and have exceptional ability and stamina. To obtain the title of Sumo, these wrestlers must put in years of effort.

Everyone on the earth has something in common with the Sumo. They must keep their equilibrium or else they will lose the contest. A Grand Champion Sumo is someone who has kept their balance better than their opponents.

He obtains public acclaim and financial advantages because of his achievements. One of the most valuable assets for a Suma is a sense of balance.

Balance is important in life as well. Without life's stability, you will also lose some battles. I would want to demonstrate the importance of balance with a humorous example. I would like you to close your eyes and envision yourself in a circus.

Now you can see two massive Sumo wrestlers balancing on a tightrope of equal weight and size. The wrestlers are high above the crowd, on opposing ends of a tightrope. Consider putting a monkey in the middle of the tightrope. Of course, everything would be in balance if the monkey stayed in the middle of the tightrope.

One of the wrestlers, though, offers the monkey a banana.

The tightrope begins to sway as the monkey approaches the banana. Even though the monkey is not particularly heavy, its movement will cause a tiny shift in the equilibrium. The now unstable sumo wrestlers will eventually tumble to a safety net as the monkey travels further to one side of the tightrope toward the banana. Life, too, may be full of drama and comedy if it is not balanced.

Something divided into equal proportions, sizes, weights, or amounts is said to be in balance. Because no one is born with the ability to balance, we must learn how to establish and maintain mental, physical, and spiritual equilibrium. Remember, like the Sumo wrestler, equilibrium is your friend and must be maintained via constant practice.

A lack of balance in your life might have a negative impact on your overall health. Balance is important for stress levels, time management, goal setting, educational attainment, and wellness. Spirituality is a critical role in maintaining life's balance, according to scientists."

The woman abruptly stopped speaking, and the lights dimmed. The Sumos came in all their magnificence, and the crowd erupted in applause! The satellites are following the Sage's every move.

Unleash Your Vision

SUCCESS IS A PERSONAL

As the sun peered through the clouds, the scent of fresh cinnamon filled the air. A local artist waited near the stage. He wanted to create a portrait of the group. Fresh ripe mangoes fell from the branches as WizdomTalk began to teach.

When the Sage pointed to the fruit and wrinkled his brows, the fruit came to a halt in mid-flight! An invisible hand then miraculously peeled and sliced the fruit. The fruit is offered by the Sage to the enthralled islanders.

Then Wizdomtalk started talking, "Isn't it true that everyone in this room aspires to be successful? But what exactly is success?

To most individuals, success entails achieving a goal. Anyone who wishes to live a successful life aspires to attain many goals.

Success is like a pineapple seed, in that if it is cultivated, it can produce more of its type. Let us travel to France, shall we?" WizdomTalk grabbed a large fishing net and threw it on the group.

The islanders arrived at the Louvre Museum in Paris as a mist cleared the air.

"What do you think about these paintings?" Wizdomtalk asked the gathering as he pointed to two paintings. Some people expressed their dissatisfaction with them. Others were uninterested, while others enjoyed them.

"If you possessed these paintings, what would you do with them?" He inquired. Some indicated they would keep them, while others said they would toss them in the trash, and yet others said they would give them away.

He continued, saying, "Your reactions to these paintings are all personal and dependent on your values and preferences. It is the same with success. What you want to do with your own life and achieve is always a personal choice. You should be able to choose whether you want to fly to the moon or plant exotic fruit.

It should be your option, the profession you choose in your life. It is up to you to decide how you want to exhibit your faith. You should have the freedom to select who you marry and what initiatives you take part in. It is up to you to choose your friends.

You should be able to choose what you wear. What form of higher education you pursue should be a personal decision as well. All the things I have mentioned are highly subjective and should be left up to you to decide.

In this regard, you should not be too concerned with what other people think of your choices. This option entails not injuring others or violating cultural taboos, religious convictions, or civil or governmental regulations. You should be able to paint your life as you see it as an artist.

The paintings you are looking at are Picasso's, and they are worth millions of dollars. To me, Robert H's portrait of our group will be valuable.

Let us take a closer look at drumbeats. It will assist you in getting closer to your goal."

WizdomTalk froze and posed for Robert H, a local artist, with a big smile on his face.

THE DRUMBEATS

The following day, the crowd expanded in size as they awaited WizdomTalk's arrival. The stage is suddenly engulfed by quiet drumming and peppermint-scented mist.

WizdomTalk arrived this time, clothed in traditional African garb. He smiled and directed his gaze to the audience.

"Rise!" he cried, wriggling his brows, and raising his arms. Everyone is mysteriously transported to Rwanda and was raised into a white cloud.

The islanders could hear loud drumming as the cloud passed over a colorful Rwanda village. They saw a young

Caucasian student dressed in traditional African attire. A massive mountain gorilla was clad in native yellow clothes and dancing to the beat of the drums.

According to WizdomTalk, "Phillip is the student's name, and he is from Iceland. He has been studying and practicing drumming on a regular basis to learn the secrets of the drumbeat. You might be wondering why this matters so much to him."

WizdomTalk yawned and appeared out of nowhere, holding a tall glass of ice-cold orange juice. He took a big sip, he froze, and then fell asleep in the middle of his lesson, smiling! The stunned islanders burst out laughing.

Glasses of cold orange juice unexpectedly fell from the skies for everyone's enjoyment! About 20 minutes later, WizdomTalk awoke. As if nothing had happened, he resumed his lesson. "As a wise man, Phillip realizes that the drumbeat's vibration and rhythm may be employed as a potent and effective tool to change healing energy," he stated.

"Depression, low self-esteem, and violence can all be treated with this therapeutic energy. Phillip and his psychologist wife, Dr. Joy, are working on a therapeutic program that will use the drum's healing capacity to help socially traumatized youngsters."

When George, the dancing Mountain Gorilla, looked up, he discovered a mob of islanders watching him. He screamed and waved his arms and said, "Hello there, friends! The drum is one of the world's oldest instruments. The drum was once used to send messages from village to village in ancient societies.

Drumming was also used in religious ceremonies, such as weddings, burials, rites of passage, and celebrations. The drumbeat's rhythm is also used in healing rituals and storytelling. The drumbeat boosts your pulse or heartbeat and reflects your own life energy. Drumbeats represent life's rhythm and velocity.

They instill sympathy in us, and the beat transcends all ethnic and linguistic boundaries.

Furthermore, the drumming is a natural healer that is extremely relaxing." George the Mountain Gorilla smiled and waved goodbye to everyone as he said this.

According to WizdomTalk, "Dr. Joy and Phillip are both DREAMMAKERS. They have concentrated on their interests. Phillip and Dr. Joy eventually received Master Drummer certification.

Thousands of rehabilitating problematic youngsters will be introduced to drumming as a therapeutic healing technique one rhythm at a time.

As we continue our teachings, keep in mind that the drumming symbolizes life. We will talk about 'Incredible Courage' tomorrow. "The crowd is following WizdomTalk's every move.

Unleash Your Vision

THE PALAUAN'S COURAGE

WizdomTalk decided to tell another story because it was lunchtime, and the islanders were restless. He started by saying, "Surangel, a fisherman slept through a brief quiet storm off the coast of Palau, a lovely South Pacific Island.

He woke up to find that his small paddle boat had been blown off course. The ship drifted miles into the open sea once the storm passed, leaving the fisher stranded and afraid.

After the Palau rescue team went home without being able to locate the man, his village assumed he had drowned. As Surangel faced the idea of never seeing his wife and children again, the guy sobbed.

As his small boat was rocked and turned by the enormous waves, he gave up all chance of being rescued.

His only wish was to die with dignity before being eaten by sharks and barracudas.

Surangel had brought a compass, food, drink, and some betel nuts to chew, as a seasoned fisherman, but his supplies would not last.

There was nothing or no one as far as his eyes could see, just miles and miles of open sea. As he chewed his betel nuts and lime, which always left a scarlet stain in his mouth, he considered dying.

He did not spot the humpback whale approaching his boat because it was quite dark, and the ocean current was loud. The gigantic whale, on the other hand, simply followed the ship in silence. The fisher begged for aid and soon fell asleep, hoping it was all a dream.

He woke up the next morning with a strong sulfur odor. He was terrified when Dark Shadows came in his boat out of nowhere. He told Dark Shadows to leave, still believing he was dreaming. The fisherman's scream could be heard for miles when Dark Shadows came over and pinched him to verify that he was genuine.

'Who are you?' he asks Dark Shadows, trembling. 'You stupid moron, I am your worst nightmare,' Dark Shadows proudly said.

Then Surangel resumed his prayer, but Dark Shadows refused to depart. With his paddle, he struck Dark Shadows, but it passed right through him, as if he were a ghost. Dark Shadows mockingly predicted that the fisherman would die soon, that his widow would remarry, and that his children would have a new father.

'Why me?' screamed Surangel. 'Really, who are you?' Dark Shadows answered with a terrible laugh, 'You are not invincible to the opposition. I am your most vehement foe. I am opposed to your success and wish for you to fail. I do not want you to realize your full potential or fulfill your destiny.'

The fisherman was not a well-educated man, and he did not really get what Dark Shadows had said. He loved his family, though, and he was aware that they were about to be taken from him.

The fisherman is enraged by this thinking. He thought to himself as he lay down to sleep. 'I need to devise a strategy and summon the courage to carry it out since my family relies on me.'

Surangel woke up alone on his third day at sea. His lips were chapped, and his skin was severely burnt. Even though Dark Shadows was no longer present, the fisherman's thoughts were haunted by his remarks. He started to reason and think to himself, and he moved his compass north.

The only other alternative for the Surangel was to hope for rescue. He was initially startled by the sight of a big humpback whale swimming near his boat. He regained his composure as he remembered his family and knew that this whale might either assist or damage him.

Out of nowhere a big wave slammed into his boat, smashing it into driftwood and hurling him into the ocean. Surangel summoned the bravery to hold the whale's fin, and he was immediately aided and directed across the sea.

Surangel would hold his breath every time the whale went underwater. The fisherman would take a breath whenever the whale came up for air.

This journey lasted for hours, yet Surangel refused to let go! When he was tired and released the whale's fin, he discovered some driftwood and began to float. When he spotted a light in the distance, he assumed he was hallucinating.

The next morning some Chuuk, Yap, Kosrae, Pohnpei, Kiribati, Nauru, and Marshall Islands students came across the sleeping Surangel on the beach. Surangel returned home to a hero's welcome, and there was a huge party on Palau's island in honor of his bravery.

The village leader told Surangel that his family and community had given up hope of ever seeing him alive again.

'Courage is built in a strong dedication to someone or something,' Surangel remarked. Smiling, he continued by saying, "My love for my family gave me the determination to never give up. Even when faced with ferocious opposition and Dark Shadows, I believed we should never forget that we have the option of using Courage. "

THE REFALUWASCH – EDUCATION

The stars shone brightly in the sky, as the breezes swept in from the north. WizdomTalk, the islanders, and their visitors came across a Refaluwasch elder named Olopai while strolling down the shore. He was grilling succulent fish outside a cabin while creating a traditional canoe with others. The elder, a well-known scholar, author, and historian, came to a halt.

He then begins to describe the culture of his people to his visitors. "The Refaluwasch, or Carolinian people, are from the eastern Caroline Islands," Elder Olopai explained. "The Relaluwasch are well-known seafarers."

Around 2,000 years ago, our ancestors may have moved from Asia and Indonesia to Micronesia. In the

Mariana Islands, the Chamorro people arrived first, followed by us. We enjoy crafts, fishing, cooking, and sailing, and we live in a matriarchal community that values respect. The Chamorro people and the Carolinian work together to establish a harmonious community."

Elder Olopai stumbled across Mr. Chen and the workers' crew while highlighting several traditional sites surrounding his village. The laborers were tanned from digging trenches along the beach in the scorching sun. Mr. Chen, a kind middle-aged married father of four, had spent 30 years digging trenches.

Mr. Chen's pay day had arrived, and he is having difficulty counting his money and reading a note from his supervisor. Mr. Chen, unfortunately, did not appreciate education as a child and was therefore illiterate. Mr. Chen, being the nice man he was, understood that all respectable labor, even digging ditches, carried honor and dignity.

"Could you please help me read an important letter from my employer?" Mr. Chen asked Elder Olopai. "Sure," said the elder. He felt sorry for Mr. Chen as he reads the letter. "We will no longer require your labor due to advanced technologies. We appreciate your 30 years of service." the letter stated.

Mr. Chen grew upset and spoke up when he was informed what the letter said. "I am uneducated! All I know how to do is dig trenches! How am I going to feed my family now?" He stared at the gathering, tears in his eyes, and angrily advised them, "Don't be like me. Learn to appreciate education."

"Knowledge and education are extremely vital and valuable," Elder Olopai remarked. "Mr. Chen is an example of someone who did not place a high priority on schooling, and his job opportunities are limited. Mr. Chen is now an adult who needs to return to school and master new skills.

Here is an example of knowledge acquisition. You are all capable of doing arithmetic and reading a book. What method did you use to learn these facts? I am confident you learned about these topics in school. When you have a good education, it can open numerous doors of opportunities. You limit your employment and income prospects if you do not know what you are doing.

Develop an interest in disciplines such as trades, science, math, reading, languages, history, geography, and the arts. Math and science education prepares you for careers in technology and medicine. Learning a language will set you apart from others by allowing you to communicate effectively with other cultures.

History and geography will teach you about the past and how it relates to the present. The performing arts, such as drama, dance, and music are just a few of the wonderful art forms to learn about. Painting, sketching, and sculpting, on the other hand, are visual arts. You might desire to acquire a degree at a university or study a trade at a technical college.

Unleash Your Vision

Education is a unique experience. Keep in mind that once you get an education, no one can take it away from you. You are never too old, and it is never too late to learn and receive an EDUCATION, my friends," said Elder Olopai.

IT IS ALL ABOUT RESPECT

Thousands of people gathered in Memorial Park in Saipan on this day to hear WizdomTalk speak. The Sage then went on to narrate another story, saying, "On a bitterly chilly day in the Netherlands, a lengthy line formed outside the Shultz Bank.

They were present during the event's grand opening. Mr. Joseph, a well-dressed businessperson, awaited his arrival anxiously. Because he was wealthy, he believed he was more important than the other clients. As a result, he advanced to the front of the queue.

He walked by an elderly woman carrying a lunch box, ignoring the other customers who were waiting. She had arrived at the bank early, anticipating a long wait, in the hopes of taking care of her business. She did not say anything about the businessman's plainly disrespectful behavior, because she was trembling from the cold.

When the bank opened, however, the older lady walked forward and informed the bank manager that she and the other customers had been waiting much longer. Because the bank manager believed Mr. Joseph was a 'more important' customer, he ignored her complaints and allowed him to be served first.

Mr. Rosenberg, a janitor, who has been working at the bank for 35-years, witnessed the scenario as he went about his work.

He approached the bank's new boss, shaking his head disapprovingly, and requested to talk with him alone. The new bank manager agreed, and the janitor arranged for him to meet the woman he had overlooked.

The janitor said, "Please allow me to present Mrs. Shultz to you. She is the bank's founder's widow. She is now the sole owner of the bank!" "Oh," said the new bank manager. The janitor continued and said, "You see, Ms. Shultz had made it a habit to deliver lunch to new managers on their first day at work, so that is the reason she was at the bank that day."

WizdomTalk continued the story and said, "The new manager was very humiliated, and he began excessively apologizing. It was, however, too late to undo the harm he had done. He was fired from his well-paying job on his first day because of his arrogance and rudeness.

You must all understand that if you want respect, you must first earn it. We earn respect by treating people with respect. Learn to be helpful, kind, and honest. Treat others in the same way that you wish to be treated in other words, "What goes around, comes around!"

The effect or outcomes you or your family will receive in the future will be determined by your current behaviors or activities you do now, whether positive or bad. Life may appear unfair at times but remember that everything that happens in your life has a purpose.

The answers to life's questions are not always straightforward. Just remember that we will always be given the life lessons of Respect. Let us now study the concept of integrity." The cameras are following the Sage's every move.

Unleash Your Vision

Integrity

Seagulls sailed high over the blue-green water, occasionally swooping down to pick up lunch, as the islanders waited. WizdomTalk stated, "Integrity is one of the most significant character attributes any one can have.

Integrity is defined as being honest and having strong moral beliefs. Selfishness and greed can lead to people seeking personal gain and fortune at the expense of their integrity in today's environment. There was a time when someone committed to do something, their word was their bond.

In other words, a person's true character was determined by their desire to perform what they stated they would do. While no one is flawless, a person of integrity strives to accomplish what they say they will do, regardless of the repercussions.

If they are unable to keep their commitment for some reason, they will let you know. A person with integrity understands the importance of trust, fairness, sincerity, and honesty WizdomTalk added.

"Please accompany me to the Harbor Fish Market. I would like you to see some of our local business procedures." As they approached a fish stand run by a local fisherman named JoJo, they were greeted with the putrid odor of a dead fish. They noticed JoJo selling bluefin tuna to the locals for $5 per kilo. When he sold fish to a visitor or tourist, however, the price was always double.

Then an international business executive approached Kilili, who worked for JoJo. He was hoping to buy fish for a meeting on the island that will feed many people. He examined the wide variety of fish on sale at the modest stall. The visitor chose the tuna. He inquired of Kilili, "How much will it cost?"

"This fellow is from a rich country, therefore charge him 15 dollars a kilo for the Bluefin tuna," Jojo, the stall's proprietor, whispered to Kilili in their native tongue before Kilili opened his lips to respond. Kilili expressed his displeasure in their language, claiming that he could not be that deceitful and unfair.

JoJo said to Kilili, "For such an enormous size, you will undoubtedly collect a large commission. You will, however, be dismissed if you believe your morality will not allow you to cheat!" Kilili had only recently married, and the owner was aware of this. He and his new wife were expecting their first kid and were in severe need of financial assistance to support their expanding family.

Kilili, however, was a fair and honest person who valued the teachings in honesty instilled in him by his Chamorro and Carolinian ancestors. With a pleasant smile, he said, "Five dollars per kilo, sir." Kilili was sacked by the irate owner shortly after the transaction was completed. Kilili's predicament was translated and communicated to the executive, by the tour leader.

The executive was taken aback and spoke to Kilili through the tourist guide. The executive gave Kilili his card and encouraged him with the help of the translator guide, by saying,

"THE WORLD NEEDS MORE PEOPLE LIKE YOU WITH INTEGRITY AND IN THE FUTURE, YOU MIGHT HAVE SUCCESS IN POLITICS!

I would like to offer you a position. Please report to my local office at 8:00 a.m. tomorrow.

It always pays off to be honest, fair, and forthright."

"Always maintain INTEGRITY! Let us now study the concept of accountability," said WizdomTalk.

Choice & Accountability

WizdomTalk was dressed professionally with a bow tie today and was using a calculator. He was impersonating an accountant. "Personal accountability is one of the most significant character traits we may have," he said to his audience. The Sage continued, "Having the requirement or willingness to bear responsibility or be answerable for one's words and deeds is referred to as accountability.

Many people are unaccountable for their conduct. Most of the time, people place blame on others for their misfortunes. You will not be able to attain major success until you, or someone else, holds you personally responsible for your activities.

Keeping promises is a vital component of being accountable. When you make a commitment, make every effort to keep it. Refuse to participate in the blame game. To put it another way, do not blame others for your errors. Accept the repercussions of your actions, even if they are not appropriate.

Unleash Your Vision

In many serious criminal cases, the defendant frequently enters a plea of not guilty. These defendants waste court resources and other people's time trying to outsmart the system. They do this even when they are aware that they have committed a crime. The fundamental reason for this is that the guilty person does not want to go to prison. In most cases, however, the defendant is found guilty."

Let us go into the park and listen in on Ms. Green's talk with her son Bobby, who is struggling in school. Bobby has always been on the honor roll in school. This is what people hear when they sit close to the mother and son."

"Bobby, how are your studies going?" Mrs. Green inquired. "Your grades have taken a hit."

"Mother, you know that I am interested in athletics and have a part-time job, so I don't have as much time to study," Bobby explained.

"Accept the consequences, even if they are unpleasant," said his mother. Bobby expressed himself to his adoring mother, "Would I be able to play sports and work next year if I improved my grades this year?" "Yes, Bobby," Mrs. Green replied.

The Sage said, "Bobby utilized extracurricular activities and the blame game as a shield and excuse, as you can see in this example. Look for someone to hold you accountable, such as mentors.

If you learn to take personal accountability seriously, you will be able to accomplish a great deal. Let us now embark on a journey to discover Excellence."

Unleash Your Vision

A BOLT OF EXCELLENCE

The ground is struck by a white lightning bolt. The group is transported back in time to a vibrant and hot Brazilian metropolis. With immense pleasure and passion, the Brazilian people hosted the Olympic Games.

WizdomTalk is situated in the middle of the massive stadium, beneath a yellow tent. "Excellence reflects both human action and character," the Sage began to teach. "The term excellence refers to having an elevated level of quality or being extraordinarily good at something, as well as achieving final merit in some endeavors.

The greatest joy in attaining brilliance extends beyond the task at hand. What matters most in any endeavor is what you learn along the way. Excellence aids people in realizing their potential.

Integrity is required to attain excellence. When you say you are going to do something, you must follow through with it. You must be dedicated and accept responsibility for what you want to do, as well as be personally accountable for the results.

When a professional soccer team wins the World Cup, they have reached the pinnacle of their sport. When a scientist wins the Nobel Prize or discovers a cure for an illness, they have reached excellence. When a corporation has a larger market share, it can achieve excellence in business.

When a person attempts to create excellent music or art, or invents something valuable, they can reach excellence.

You can be guided in the direction of reaching excellence in your life by being the finest parent, employee, volunteer, or community leader. Excellence can be attained in one's personal life by getting a higher education degree or a greater level of expertise in a trade. Healthy food, exercise, and pursuing mental and emotional balance in life are all ways to improve one's health, and that is excellence.

People who achieve success in several areas of their lives learn to be adaptable. These folks communicate with excellent intentions and a sense of purpose in other people's lives. People who achieve excellence recognize that failure may lead to achievement and learn from their mistakes. Let us now witness excellence in action through the lens of a bolt of lightning."

The party is transported to the track and field arena as they were going to figure out what WizdomTalk meant. As the enormous throng waited for the sculpted athletes to appear, a quiet fell over them. The audience erupted in applause as each athlete and the country they represented was introduced. The race began. A Jamaican athlete rushed across the finish line in the blink of an eye.

The Sage said, "To get to the Olympics, this world-class athlete followed all the guidelines and earned numerous gold medals. Surely, that was a bolt of brilliance, and the audience went insane, yelling, "USAIN!!!"

"Let us now comprehend the power of Compassion." The cameras are following the Sage's every move.

OUR COMPASSION

The islanders and youth summit attendees were seeing the big-screen monitor on stage on this day. They were looking at the congested streets of Kolkata, India, which bustled with scooters and autos.

The majestic Taj Mahal and Mother Teresa were both found in this gorgeous country with a population of over a billion people. "Would you like to visit India?" WizdomTalk asked the audience. "Yes," they exclaimed.

"Everyone should close their eyes and count to five," according to WizdomTalk. He wiggled his dimples and brows, and his cap was tilted to the side. Suddenly, they saw Mother Teresa's office and the Missionaries of Charity in Kolkata were flooded with people.

The Sage added, "You couldn't help but adore Mother Teresa, regardless of your religious faith. She was awarded the Nobel Peace Prize for her charitable work with her organization." The atmosphere was full of compassion as the audience entered the Missionaries of Charity orphanages! It was palpable in the air! The nuns and foreign volunteers shared acts of kindness wherever the group traveled."

The group traveled through the botanical garden during their visit and saw an elderly couple being cared for by two young children. "What is compassion?" WizdomTalk asked the audience. "Being good to your family and your community," someone answered.

"Yes, that is right," WizdomTalk responded, "but there is more!" The Sage said, "The term COMPASSION comes from the word passion, which denotes a fervent desire for something. Compassion is an emotion that arises in reaction to other people's suffering and drives us to want to help them.

Showing compassion towards relatives and friends is quite easy. Compassion towards strangers, on the other hand, needs more effort and comprehension of its genuine meaning. Compassion is more than just empathy; it often leads to a desire to help others who are suffering. The world would be a cold, self-centered place without acts of compassion and displays of enthusiasm.

You can show compassion for the environment by respecting by doing things like recycling and avoiding polluting the air and streams. By respecting others' ideas and refraining from unnecessary confrontations or acts of violence, you can demonstrate compassion for the dignity of life. You can show compassion for the elderly by respecting and protecting their wisdom and values.

You can have a fervent desire to learn. Our knowledge allows us to see how everything is interconnected and interdependent. One of the highest expressions of compassion we can make is an act of mercy and loving-kindness directed towards others who are less fortunate than ourselves.

Compassion can also be demonstrated through caring for and helping in the creation of laws to safeguard the rights of domestic and wild animals. By developing, honoring, and protecting each generation, you can have a passion and love for your family.

Furthermore, we must respect, esteem, and acknowledge the dignity of people who are mentally or physically handicapped. By embracing diversity, you may demonstrate your commitment to your community. Take steps to make your neighborhood a safer place to live. Compassion is essential for our physical and emotional well-being.

Finally, kindness can be a passion for you!!! We urge those around us to do the same by setting an example and performing acts of kindness in our homes, workplaces, and communities. As a result, demonstrating that a loving, tolerant, and just world full of stewardship is attainable," WizdomTalk said.

PRACTICE STEWARDSHIP

WizdomTalk was standing near a massive helicopter pad, talking to himself, when he was discovered by a bunch of islanders. He invited them for a ride right away on the helicopter. They talked passionately as they glided above the water. They witnessed a ship dumping toxic waste when the helicopter hovered over it.

WizdomTalk took advantage of the situation and began speaking. He, then dozed off and fell from the helicopter into the frigid ocean. A pod of massive humpback whales somehow plucked the Sage from the ocean. They assumed positions and formed a ladder towards the hovering vessel, allowing him to climb to safety. Each whale felt sorry for the Sage.

Finally, Save Us, a female whale, reached the helicopter's door. She led the appreciative Sage to safely re-enter the helicopter. When Save Us opened her lips, the group was terrified, but all she did was spit warm water all over them. It was her way of greeting them.

Surprisingly, Save Us began to talk with and educate the islanders. She said, "Stewardship is the process of managing and protecting resources, and it is a responsibility that we all share. We should all naturally feel responsible for humanity's and the world's common welfare.

The result of good stewardship is a management style that conserves, preserves, and multiplies resources. Poor stewardship is a selfish, self-centered management style that results in waste and devastation.

Even though the world has enough resources to suit the requirements of all its inhabitants, selfishness and a lack of adequate stewardship have complicated matters.

Let us have a look at an example. Trees provide oxygen to our environment, yet they are increasingly being destroyed. Trees are reduced on a global basis, resulting in deforestation. The world's oceans have grown contaminated because of the dumping of waste and harmful chemicals.

Toxic air pollution is destroying the ozone layer across the planet, especially in most urban places. The layer protects the earth from the sun's damaging rays and is necessary for life to exist on the planet.

Animal species have become endangered because of human poaching and degradation of rainforest environments. Women, children, and the elderly, who are among your most vulnerable are being abused." Save Us went silent and dove back into the water.

WizdomTalk stated, "Fortunately, there are many brave people, groups, and policies committed to tackling these concerns. To help safeguard and save our world, we must all play our part in practicing good stewardship.

Let us continue Stewardship in our communities or get started!" The youth continued to watch through the internet and television.

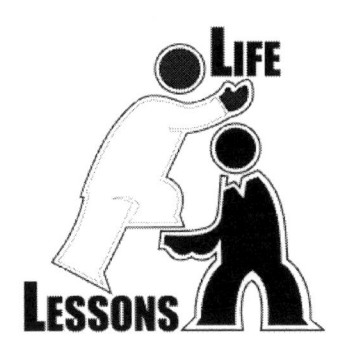

SOMETHING GREATER THAN YOU?

As the crowd and youth summit attendees built a massive campfire and began roasting their food, the sky lit up with bright white shooting stars.

Sheba a philosophy student, questioned WizdomTalk. "Why am I here? How am I related to the world around me?" Sheba's inquiries stemmed from a recent article she had read about a momentous World Peace Conference.

Three world superpowers—China, Russia, and the United States—hosted the event in Vienna, Austria.

WizdomTalk responded, "Each nation maintains affluent economies, powerful military defense forces, and a slew of highly educated advisors. They could not come to an agreement on how to create global peace.

Most of their leaders appeared to be more concerned with restraining small groups of terrorists who threatened to use biochemical and nuclear weapons to destroy the globe.

Each of these heads of state was clearly competing against each other. Based on their own self-interests, each leader wanted to play a prominent role in determining the world's destiny. World peace was a subjective ideal for each leader. They rapidly realized that each country's notion of peace and the road to achieving it were distinct.

For example, under the pretense of promoting peace, foreign forces exercised dominance and control. Each leader boasted about developing a plan for world peace at the press conference that followed the summit.

Fortunately, one of the leaders became exhausted after answering the questions posed by reporters, as he was attempting to divert the attention of these seasoned professionals. The Head of State grabbed a young reporter he thought would not ask any tough questions and gave him two questions to ask and one comment.

Zaldy, a representative of the Marianas Variety, a Filipino youth reporter, is overjoyed to have been summoned to participate but he tripped and began to stutter."

"If you-you leaders are so influential, why –why do two billion people around the world lack clean water?" Zaldy asked. He also inquired "If you-you world powers are like elephants in a room, and world peace is like mice, then why can't you, leaders, and the peoples of the globe accomplish world - world peace?"

The Sage continued, "Seeing that this highly clever but awkward little guy was searching for answers, the leaders urged him to answer his own questions.

Just as Zaldy was gathering his strength and about to respond to the leaders, two white birds appeared and landed on his shoulders.

The audience and the leaders were both taken aback. The lovely doves were remarkable in stature and grace, and they exuded wisdom. "Please, Zaldy, let me assist you in answering these questions," one dove offered.

" Yes, sure, sure," Zaldy answered, stuttering.

The dove spoke. "World peace can begin right here with us. The answer is in gaining a better knowledge of what we cannot see. That is our spiritual or pure nature.

The world's nations and peoples must learn to treat others, animals, and the environment with more compassion, morality, fairness, tolerance, stewardship, accountability, and understanding. These characteristics are founded on spirituality, regardless of a person's nationality or culture.

Please keep in mind that the animal kingdom does not use all these characteristics; only humans do. Compassion and tolerance are sometimes shown by animals, but never morality, fairness, stewardship, accountability, or comprehension. Consider the following scenario.

When was the last time you witnessed a crocodile purposefully share its meal with other hungry animals? They normally do not because they are driven by instincts and lack a sense of fairness and, occasionally, sympathy for others.

I do not mean religion when I speak of spirituality.

There is a distinction. People's spiritual lives are intertwined with their affiliation with a church, temple, mosque, or synagogue. Others may turn to prayer or a personal relationship with God or a higher force for comfort. Others look for significance in life through their relationships with nature or art.

Your sense of purpose, as well as your understanding of spirituality, can shift throughout time as you adjust to new experiences and relationships. However, I believe we can all agree that what we truly desire is happiness!

Only by evaluating what spirituality means in each of our lives, seeking it through our best knowledge, and doing good acts will we be able to actualize it. Because our lives and our environment are inextricably linked."

The dove paused in its speech, turned to face the heavens, smiled, and nodded. Then the two doves took off into the sky. The Sage sighed as he concluded his recount of what happened at the conference. The satellites are following the Sage's every move.

YOU ARE A BRAND

Brown coconuts fell from the trees and broke open as huge gusts and waves approached the shore. As they ate a nice snack, the islanders and their visitors were overjoyed.

WizdomTalk met the crowd later in the day, and they walked by a JoeTen department store and peered through its window. They kept an eye on customers who were shopping for the most recent deals. Some were buying food, toys, while others were buying technology.

A large green box with a ribbon on it sat in the middle of the floor. "A BRAND-NEW ME," read the ribbon. "What does this box represent, and why is it here?" Rochelle inquired of the Sage.

Unleash Your Vision

The green box suddenly unwrapped itself, stood up, and came to life. Rochelle and the rest of the crowd were taken aback. "Rochelle, "A BRAND-NEW ME is an advertising slogan," the box said as it approached the group at the window. The green box continued and said, "It implies that buyers are feeling brand new and need to purchase items that complement their new appearance.

The motto, however, has another hidden meaning that only enlightened people are aware of. The term 'brand' is commonly used in the business world. A company's brand is how it distinguishes itself, and it will go to considerable efforts to protect and promote it.

But what exactly is a company's brand? A brand is a marketing strategy that involves the creation of a name, symbol, or design that identifies and distinguishes a service or product. In an increasingly competitive market, having a strong brand strategy gives you a substantial competitive advantage.

A Mercedes Benz vehicle, for example, is a brand of automobile. Quaker Oats is a cereal brand. Calvin Klein is a clothing line. Emirates Airlines is a company that provides air transportation. Manchester United is a soccer team's brand. The Beatles are a singing group with a well-known brand. Musicians, artists, actors, comedians, and athletes are frequently viewed as brands.

You are ready to move forward with your business and branding plan once you have defined your brand and chosen a name. A genuine DREAMMAKER is both a worker and a consumer, as well as someone who engages in commerce to generate many sources of revenue.

Aside from having a job or a profession, to prosper financially and construct a secure future for yourself and your family, you must be an investor, a product producer, or give a public service.

Building a brand, sharing a website, promoting your business, and informing others about what you do are all fantastic uses of social media. Building a brand is a continuous process that requires you to publicize your brand's successes and accomplishments.

Mail is used to communicate with potential clients and customers; the internet and social media are also important. You should always attempt to create positive conversations and impressions of your company that set it apart from the competition," explained the green box.

The green box rewrapped itself, stood steady, and went silent without warning. The visitors re-examined the large box and the ribbon that read, "A Brand-New Me," and finally realized the brand's hidden meaning.

Unleash Your Vision

THE DEBT CHAINS

A beautiful rainbow appeared in the sky when the rain stopped. At the local community hall, WizdomTalk exposed the islanders and guests to The Debtbusters. They drove to the homeless and vagrant people's homes after the introduction. The filthy odors pervaded the desolate, decaying structures.

When they passed an abandoned vehicle, they realized that it was being used as a refuge for a family. Mr. Debtbusters got off the bus, walked down the aisle, and knocked on the door.

Mr. Debtbusters stated, "Meet the Brokers. Once upon a time, the Brokers were a typical middle-class family with good employment and lived in a great area.

Unlike some unskilled homeless persons, the Brokers are well-educated and talented," Mr. Debtbusters continued.

"The Brokers, unfortunately, had a severe problem. OVERSPENDING! They had no savings when their income decreased due to a change in the economy. As a result, they were unable to pay their expenses and lost everything they owned. The Brokers are now wallowing in self-pity and blaming others for their woes. They now live in their car and rely on the kindness of others for meals.

Imagine walking around with a 50-kilogram ball and chain around your neck," Mrs. Debtbusters stated as she took over the lecture.

She said, "These weights are undetectable by the naked eye. You are not aware of it because your parents and ancestors wore the same ball and chain, and you assumed it was just part of life.

What if 70% of the people around you were wearing a 'consumer debt' ball and chain around their necks? Most people would be startled and appalled, but this is occurring across the world. The balls and chains are completely undetectable.

The discomfort and persistent tension they cause, however, are real. DEBT is a ball and chain that affects the lives of individuals as well as entire nations. When people could not pay their debts less than a century ago, they were placed in jail. This punishment is still in place in nations today.

In several countries less than two hundred years ago, if you did not pay your debt, you could have been forced to become an indentured servant or slave.

Personal debt can become a type of enslavement, resulting in conflict and the eventual disintegration of a solid family. People frequently become in debt because of their inability to manage their finances. Today's consumption is out of hand!

Individuals are in tremendous debt due to their inability to wait for gratification. In other words, even though they lack the financial means to do so, they spend to keep up with the current trend, style, or perceived image of their neighbors.

Commercials that are seductive add to the problem by influencing people's values and purchasing patterns. If left uncontrolled, this style of spending can lead to a life focused solely on consumption rather than production.

If you are drowning in debt, you will not be able to develop wealth. Before you buy something, it is a good practice to ask yourself if you really need it. 'Is there anything I already have that could serve as a replacement?' Is it possible that a good secondhand item will suffice?

Now is the moment to start saving money and effectively utilizing your resources in preparation for your later years," said Mrs. Debtbusters.

WizdomTalk said, "Never forget the Brokers, because you don't want to end up like them—BROKE." The people expressed their gratitude to the Debtbusters as they reflected on the lesson they have learned.

Unleash Your Vision

RECOGNIZE WEALTH AROUND YOU

The weather the next day was beautiful and moderate, providing the ideal conditions for learning. The General and WizdomTalk greeted the islanders and guests at The People's Bank. The group then boarded a large blue bus that whisked them across the ocean to Guam's island.

The cameras were following WizdomTalk's every move, and the Youth Summit participants were watching. The group arrived at the Man'amko Retirement Center after landing. The retirement community was huge and lovely, and the inhabitants were content.

The senior people were known as "Man'amko," and they worked in the gardens while the rest of the residents' played games and had fun. The Saipan group joined in the festivities, handing out balloons and sweets to the elderly citizens.

The youngsters were eventually escorted by the General to an exceedingly attractive couple. They were known as the Megabucks, but he introduced them as the Calvos. The Calvos had grown up in a working-class family and married when they were young.

They grew extremely affluent throughout time because of their foresight, knowledge, and challenging work. The huge Man'amko Retirement Center is now owned by the Megabucks.

The Megabucks addressed the crowd, saying, "There is a concept known as personal wealth. Personal Wealth can be accumulated through your labor or employment, or through the revenues of a business enterprise.

Inherited Wealth, on the other hand, is a type of wealth that is passed down from generation to generation. This is money that has been passed down through the centuries to be distributed to surviving family members.

Wealth acquired from property, savings, or a business inherited from parents or grandparents to benefit a family member is an example of this.

If you are a creative person, you could be able to benefit from something known as Innovative wealth. Royalties or patents earned from creating or inventing public-use products or services provide capital. An innovator who invents and patents a drone that delivers packages is an example of this.

When a songwriter writes a fresh lyric for a song that becomes popular afterwards, they are paid royalties, which is a fancy way of expressing that they are compensated for every time the song is played. This is another example of wealth created through innovation. Every country has Community Wealth. It is derived from a country's resources that benefits everyone who lives there. Saudi Arabia's oil production is an example.

Other examples include fishing and farming, minerals, plants, crafts, technologies, and skilled labor. There is also a concept known as Associated Wealth. It is the richness that comes from being associated with a well-known person, country, community, business, organization, school, or industry. Associating with someone or an organization who is prominent or with someone from another country who may be a member of the royal family is an illustration of this.

There are also Charitable Riches, which is a type of wealth. Individuals or organizations have left legacies through foundations, charity trusts, and endowments, and these assets emanate from them. It offers grants, loans, and seed money for a variety of objectives and projects, such as business development and educational scholarships.

This gets us to the most important aspect of wealth – Health Wealth. It comes from leading a healthy lifestyle, which contributes to a healthy mind and body. If someone has the drive and stamina to contribute to society throughout and into later life stages, this example is required.

Think about each category that has been offered here. All around us, treasure and money abound. You, too, may learn how to gain access to these wealth-generating sectors." The Megabucks concluded.

The group was taken aback. The appreciative islanders and guests expressed their gratitude for what was shared as well as their newly acquired knowledge.

Unleash Your Vision

LIFE'S ABCDS!

Although the day was dreary and rainy, the aroma of exotic green and yellow flowers filled the air. WizdomTalk had invited islanders and guests to meet him at Mount Carmel Cemetery. On Saipan, the old burial ground is in the village of Chana Kanoa.

Many people were apprehensive about visiting the tomb. As a child and a 40-year-old lady were laid to rest, sadness and loss were all around us. The woman died prematurely from health difficulties, even though her death may have been prevented. Sage was in tears because, while not knowing the families of the departed, he felt compassion and sympathy for them.

The islanders were perplexed when a big letter chart materialized out of nowhere in the sky. WizdomTalk stated, "All significant languages in the world have an alphabet," Letters are important because they are used to form words, phrases, and ideas.

The letters A, B, C, and D are the first four letters of the English alphabet. I am going to utilize these letters to teach you a lesson in life.

The letter A. represents your acts and activities. To manage all facets of life, you must take initiative-taking measures. Relationships, faith, health, finances, education, and community are all part of it. Your beliefs and behavior are represented by the letter B. Your character and your choices are represented by the letter C.

The Dark Shadows who will oppose your life are represented by the letter D.

Charlotte, for example, is a 40-year-old lady who is lovely but quite heavy. She stands five feet and six inches tall and weighs 350 pounds. She has worked as an accountant for the past 20 years. Sweets and carbs make up much of her diet, with very few fruits and vegetables. Her job is sedentary, and she does not get a lot of exercise there.

Charlotte prefers to spend her free time watching television rather than exercising. As a result of her excessive weight, she has a slew of health issues.

Charlotte's doctor told her at a routine checkup that if she kept up her current lifestyle, she would not survive much longer. Charlotte was upset by this, but she recognized that she must make a major life-changing decision shortly. She believed she will never be able to reduce weight because she has failed at every fad diet she has tried.

Charlotte ate a large scoop of ice cream and chocolate cake later that evening. She ate sweets as a comfort meal all the time, especially when she was stressed or depressed about something.

Charlotte's mind was invaded by Dark Shadows, ensuring that she thoroughly enjoyed the dessert.

Despite reading literature and seeking advice about her health problems, she did not take any measures or activities to improve her habit. Dark Shadows' voice torments her whenever she tries to eat healthily or exercise, assuring her that she will fail, and she believes him.

Charlotte was confronted with a circumstance to which she had no choice but to respond. To avoid any grave consequences, the situation necessitated immediate action. Charlotte's belief that she could not reduce weight was based on her failures in the past.

As a result, she was unable to make the essential changes. Do you have a similar outlook on things in your life? Charlotte's problem was losing weight and maintaining a healthy lifestyle. Which one is it for you?

Regrettably, she expects her position to improve without her making any effort. Her true option was to do nothing meaningful to improve her circumstances. She expects the status to change without her having to do anything. Do you anticipate the same outcome?

Charlotte had a major heart attack while at work one day. She was brought to the hospital by ambulance and was semi-conscious. The ambulance came to a complete stop at the Mount Carmel Cemetery. She stared at a gravestone of a woman who had died at the age of forty.

Charlotte was immediately overcome with grief as she considered her situation.

Charlotte had a fortuitous reversal as her feelings gave way to a sudden burst of courage and determination to effect change. She began praying for faith on her deathbed. She promised herself that if given the chance, she would change her way of life.

Unfortunately, Charlotte's ability to speak and walk will take several weeks due to a big stroke. Charlotte followed through on her pledge to herself and began eating a more nutritious diet.

She eventually started exercising, and over the course of two years, she shed two hundred pounds. Charlotte's self-esteem, confidence, and general outlook on life have all improved because of this significant physical alteration.

Her internal mental and spiritual metamorphosis became visible. Her body transformed into the lovely lady she was destined to be. Most crucially, Dark Shadows began to visit her less frequently.

Charlotte was wise in realizing that Dark Shadows is a violent, negative force in her life. It is possible that the 40-year-old lady they are burying today could have been Charlotte.

Please do not allow yourself to die prematurely because you were unable to overcome problems in your life that you could have avoided. Now let us all sing A, B, C, D." Then the Sage became silent.

HOW DO I HAVE PROSPERITY?

It was a strange day today. The sky was a golden hue rather than a bright blue. The clouds continued to hang above the green mountains. As the audience began to relax, WizdomTalk asked if anyone had any questions. The crowd's overwhelming response was, "How do I have prosperity?"

WizdomTalk smiled, yawned, knelt, and dozed off for a moment. With a small gray cannon in one hand and a yellow clock in the other, the Sage awoke and murmured, "So, you want to amass a hefty sum of money?"

"Of course," cried the audience. WizdomTalk set the clock aside and pulled the trigger on the cannon, aiming it at the sky. The tiny cannonball flew through the golden sky and bursts. Gold nuggets, diamonds, pearls, and money began to fall into the crowd gradually.

For five minutes, the mob went insane, collecting these goods in mass jubilation. All these valuable items then simply vanished. The group is depressed.

WizdomTalk stated, "Let us be practical. It is not easy to amass wealth. There is, however, a formula for accumulating wealth and achieving financial independence. You and your family can leave a legacy by amassing wealth. It has the potential to allow you to live a debt-free luxury lifestyle.

You can be charitable and aid others in need if you have a lot of resources. Every human has the gift to live for 24 hours a day, according to the Creator. The way a rich person uses his or her time, knowledge, talents, ambitions, and energy distinguish him or her from a poor person."

"Have you visited Stinky Island?" "No!" yelled the group.

WizdomTalk suggested, "Let us go travel and see Tan Lu, the Multibillionaire who lives in Hong Kong" The Sage clicked his fingers, and Tan Lu the Multibillionaire appeared on a gigantic screen.

The crowd was taken aback by Tan Lu's youth, as he was just in his mid-thirties. The audience was expecting someone older. His office was on Stinky Island, off the coast of Singapore, which was full of foul-smelling trash.

The Sage said, "Tan Lu was raised in an extremely poor family with no formal education. His family was certainly not associated with powerful people, so they had no one to assist them in times of need. Tan Lu from an early age, decided that he had to find a way out of poverty.

With his innovative mind and creative thinking, he invented a garbage disposal technology that was both efficient and environmentally friendly, and made a fortune from it, because his inventions were applied in a variety of locations around the world."

Tan Lu stated to the crowd, "WizdomTalk has imparted, via his lectures, that you are wealthy with intelligence, talent, and personal power, but you must use it. Your thoughts on money and prosperity, whether positive or negative, are shaped by your family, peers, and surroundings."

People aspire to be wealthy in terms of material goods and money. Wealth, however, is a subjective concept. The quantity of money one wishes to accumulate in their lifetime is a personal decision. A sheepherder in Russia with one hundred sheep may believe that if he had 10,000 sheep, he would be affluent. Another person in South America, on the other hand, may believe that they would be wealthy if they had a hundred million pesos.

Some people are born into money, while others, like me, are self-made. To acquire their money, some wealthy people conducted unscrupulous actions. Most wealthy people, on the other hand, have amassed vast sums of money in a creative and honest manner.

Spirituality, excellent character, good health, and loving relationships should never be substituted for wealth. Please do not waste your time seeking money. Money will follow you if you solely look for needs and issues to solve in the marketplace.

Here is a method to help you achieve your financial goals. Many people with noble intentions will struggle to increase their money, and the vast majority will fail. You will, in fact, have an edge if you learn the steps.

The following is the formula for accumulating more riches in your life:

1. Imagine yourself as a wealthy individual.

2. Visualize yourself in a business or hobby that you desire to pursue.

3. Launch a product, service, or talent as an entrepreneur, inventor, investor, or promoter.

4. In the marketplace, look for a need or an issue to fix.

5. Based on the need or problem you uncover, create, and brand a firm.

6. Assemble a qualified, trustworthy team to support you with money, marketing, and organization.

7. Look for resources in other people's Personal Wealth, Associated Wealth, or Community Wealth.

8. Make your product or service publicly available.

9. Automate your firm with an internet presence that can generate global sales.

10. Make a charitable contribution to your community.

Here is an easy example. Della lives in Haiti and works as a tailor, earning little money. As a hobby, she enjoys growing herbs in her modest garden.

Della was also able to tap into Associated Wealth by partnering and planting more tea leaves on a huge plot of land owned by her neighbor. She started making tea bags out of her herb leaves, which she sells in her community.

Della's tea is said to provide health benefits by many of her customers. They began to share their tea with local and international friends. Della makes a living from her local tea shop. She does, however, wish to sell her wares to a larger clientele. Even though she has no idea how to accomplish this goal.

I am going to take a break here and come back to talk about Della later.

Being employed is in no way a terrible thing. However, you have inquired as to how you can get wealthy. It will not come from working for someone if you want to be wealthy. In most circumstances, employment equals time, production, and remuneration, and these are always restricted.

You may have or be able to attain an amazing job with a good income and benefits. Even so, most people who labor for others will never become wealthy.

This is because your pay is determined by how valuable you are to the organization and the employment market. The people who put in the most physical effort are the ones who get paid the least. Professionals and competent tradespeople who employ their intellect are compensated more.

Others, such as literary, artistic, or technical scientists, performing artists, or other exceptional persons who apply their talents, are occasionally well compensated.

Professional athletes and others who have achieved celebrity status are the only exceptions to this rule. They are all members of a team, and they all have the same goal: to win tournaments. Why are certain athletes paid astronomically large sums of money while others are not?

Because of their perceived importance.

If you are an average person, you must be a distinctive marketer of a product, service, or talent, as well as an entrepreneur, developer, and investor.

You must identify a genuine need, position yourself as an analytical person in the marketplace, and build a business around it. You should keep your plans for your business ideas to a small group of people you trust. "Loose mouths sink ships," as the old saying goes.

This implies that you must pay attention to the marketplace and determine what people or communities require. You must conduct your own investigation. If you have any competition, you must learn how they operate and adjust to their business strategy or modify yours.

This will aid you in the creation of your own company strategy. Do not worry if you do not have enough money to start your business. People with money are always looking for something or someone to invest in.

Even so, your business presentation to investors should be well-researched and factually correct. It needs to be delivered with zeal and sincerity. Never give investors a larger stake in your company than you have.

Even if you are a worker and you are not an entrepreneur and you have the expertise to address important challenges at your corporate work, you can use this information to negotiate a better wage.

You could also work for a small company, because if your problem-solving enhances their business, you may be able to become a part-owner of that company or establish your own.

Remember that owning a business does not always imply that you will be wealthy. You may make a decent living or have enough money to get by, but it does not ensure the level of success you desire.

Learning how to multiply your business market with automation technology and an online presence is key to making your business a success.

To put it another way, your company must generate revenue whether you are awake, asleep, or on vacation. You must make it available to the entire globe via the internet, rather than limiting it to your town or country.

Let us return to the Della tea business dream to learn about the possibility for wealth. Della will have to conduct research and compile a list of her teas verified herbal properties. She must form a legal company, assemble a support staff, develop a business plan, and brand her organization. Her product's packaging must be one-of-a-kind.

Della needs to build a practical philosophy for her product development. She must develop a presentation on her company that discusses potential revenues, jobs, and outsourced services to local businesses, as well as the influence of the business on her neighborhood. This presentation will aid her in locating investors who can help her expand her firm with funding.

Della also must build a sales channel of wholesalers and direct salespeople that believe in her business philosophy and products. Della can start by contacting those who have used her teas in the past, both locally and in other communities.

She can establish a consumer base, starting with them, by capitalizing on this fact. Finally, Della must advertise her items to provide wealth-building chances for her distributors and direct salespeople. Della must continue to provide high-quality products to meet the expectations of her customers.

You and Della will be well on your way to accumulating more wealth if you follow this formula. This recipe for success can be used for any product or service you provide to the market. How do I smell now?" says Tan Lu. "Stinking Good," exclaimed the audience.

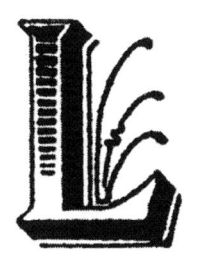

LIFE'S "L" FACTORS

The air was heavy and steamy in Santiago, Dominican Republic. WizdomTalk used television and the internet to direct islanders and World Summit Youth 20/25 members to the Eduardo León Jimenes Cultural Center for the Spoken Word event.

Portraits of prominent writers from throughout the world adorned the red brick walls. One amazing poet after another took the stage, each with their own unique style of spoken word.

Some of the poems were romantic, while others were tragic, and still others were pure comedy. The host asked inexperienced poets from the audience to take the mic and perform.

WizdomTalk went onto the stage with a smile on his face. WizdomTalk began to speak with a tilt of his cap and a wiggle of his dimples. The Sage said, "First and foremost, I'd want to express my gratitude to the Eduardo León Jimenes Cultural Center for giving me the opportunity to read my poetry.

I would like to thank my global audience, particularly young people, for listening. This poem is dedicated to the participants of the World Youth Summit 20/25 and future world leaders.

The L Factor is an important notion in one's life. The L is a powerful instrument that can be used in everyday life. This poetry, which I am about to offer, is quite remarkable. Please put this poem into practice in your life." The crowd prepared themselves for the novice poet as the lights dimmed. The Sage stood up and spoke,

The LIFE'S L's FACTORS

This L stands for LOVE and compassion for yourself and others.

This L stands for LIVING and fully experiencing one's dreams.

This L stands for LEARNING from education, life lessons, and adversity.

This L stands for LEADING yourself and others with integrity and responsibility.

This L is for LETTING GO of guilt, shame, and condemnation.

This L is for LEAVING old mistakes, unfavorable situations, and relationships behind.

This L stands for LAWS, and it refers to the impact of actions and consequences in your life.

This L stands for LEVERAGING your spirituality with your family, life, and career.

This L stands for LEGACY, which you should establish for your family and society in general."

The satellites are following the Sage's every move.

all lives matter

The Sage thanked the audience in Santiago for listening again after he finished speaking. Then he wrinkled his nose and raised his finger to the sky. He was whisked back to the Mariana Islands Festival in an instant.

WizdomTalk returned on to the island stage, dancing the cha-cha-cha. Today was WizdomTalk's final day of speaking, and the crowd was enormous. He hugged and thanked his admirers and political leaders for their time, patience, hospitality, and kindness.

He then exhorted them all to try to be the best version of themselves! WizdomTalk hugged Major General Bain his host and protégé. He thanked him for his support and wished him well. "Continue, soldier!" he saluted the General with tears in his eyes.

Unleash Your Vision

This was WizdomTalk's final lecture. He said softly and lovingly. "My dear, dear, friends and DREAMMAKERS, you now have the knowledge and capacity to dream big and achieve your goals.

You will have a positive impact on those around you as you create excellent and helpful situations in your lives, and the world will be a better place because of your example.

I shall undoubtedly miss each one of you. You have all been accepted into the exclusive DREAMMAKERS CLUB! This club is driven by faith, vision, and creativity.

An old camel is usually smarter than a young goat!" WizdomTalk stated as they parted ways. Because of their meetings with the Sage, the crowd enthusiastically nodded their agreement.

They had now grasped the significance of the parable. Then, amazingly, the Sage disappeared and appeared at the Valley of Kings at the Youth Summit, in person.

The youth went wild with excitement. WizdomTalk's eyes welled up with tears as he asked the Summit's youth to raise their lovely gift bags over their heads.

The Sage then raised his eyes to the heavens, pleading silently with The Most High, the Creator, for assistance in eradicating the Meta-Mutate Pandemic-25. Then WizdomTalk expressed gratitude to the Most High for his wisdom and power.

He then requested that some members of the crowd swiftly bring him lemons, ginger, onions, mangoes, sea salt, water, sugar, cinnamon, coconut tree bark, frankincense, and soap. He combined the ingredients in various portions and stirred them together.

WizdomTalk suddenly started blowing colorful bubbles towards the Valley of the Kings, obliterating the timed-release Meta-Mutate Pandemic -25 danger.

"You are all Dreammakers," WizdomTalk remarked, looking out over the crowd. "Now! Unleash Your Imagination."

WizdomTalk waved a flag that reads, "ALL LIVES MATTER," before freezing in place.

He smiled as he drifted off to sleep and began to snore. Then, mysteriously, WizdomTalk vanished in a cloud of peppermint fragrance.

The Babylonian Cartel, Dark Shadows, the Prime Minister, and El Marco were all horrified by what WizdomTalk had done. Their intentions had failed and there was nothing they could do about it. The agendas of Dark Shadows and his adherents unfortunately are continual, persistent, and would never stop.

Unleash Your Vision

ABOUT THE AUTHOR

Prince Chazaq is Charles Chazaq Grayer's pen name. Prince Chazaq is the author of three books: "WizdomTalk, the DreamMaker, Unleash Your Vision" and "A Day with Wizdom, Discover the Treasure in You" and "Cease Fire – Civil War, The Final Call to Redeem America." These youth and adult oriented novels, plays, and workshops reflect the author's experiences as a troubled youth, world traveler and a former director of the John F. Kennedy Center involved in international social development.

Prince Chazaq is a visionary, leader, humanitarian, entrepreneur, and former member of a paramilitary organization. The author has a hilarious and engaging method to teach character education, and self-development skills. The author is available for public speaking engagements, workshops, and coaching. Please contact him at dreammakerclub.org

Unleash Your Vision

DreamMakerclub.org

Made in the USA
Columbia, SC
21 May 2025